TOSSING THE TIARA

Keys to Creating
Powerful Women Leaders

Jeanne Martinson, MA

WOOD DRAGON BOOKS

Tossing the Tiara – Keys to Creating Powerful Women Leaders
By Jeanne Martinson, MA
Copyright 2015 by Jeanne Martinson

Wood Dragon Books
www.wooddragonbooks.com
P.O. Box 1216, Regina, Saskatchewan, Canada S4P3B4
Telephone +1.306.569.0388

ISBN:978-0-9948700-3-2

First Printing: September 2015
Second Printing: February 2016

DEDICATION

To my mom

Velma Jean Martinson

ACKNOWLEDGEMENTS

First I need to thank my husband, Malcolm. As an editor on every one of my books, he has always had a wicked eye for catching errors in grammar. He credits his Grade 13 Ontario education so here's to whoever his long ago English teacher was!

Thanks to Laurelie Martinson, my sister, who understands my work so well she can give me insight into the many ways I can take it to the next level.

Thanks to Cindy Hauck, for her sharp eye for punctuation and spelling errors.

Lastly, thank you to my friends and colleagues within BPW (Business and Professional Women) who helped shape the content of this book with your questions and curiosity.

TABLE OF CONTENTS

PART FOUR

PART FIVE

INTRODUCTION

In the introduction of my first book, "Lies and Fairy Tales That Deny Women Happiness", I wrote:

"After fifteen years of working in the area of women's issues, I have come to realize the most powerful determinants to a woman's success ... are not in legislation or employment equity policy, but in her own attitudes, beliefs and actions. Our beliefs and actions are rooted in the learnings we absorbed in the earliest years of our lives - years when we listened to fairy tales.

As we grew older, we took on the beliefs of those around us and the lies took root. These ways of believing can prevent women from enjoying the healthy relationships, satisfying careers and mental serenity that is theirs by divine right. This book explores the lies and fairy tales that deny women the path to happiness."

Much has changed positively for women in the past fifteen years, and yet in many ways we have regressed in our goals of equity.

Not only has fairy tale and myth continued to play a major part in how women view themselves and their lives, media has taken an increasing role in affecting how both men and women perceive women.

Fifteen years ago, I wrote:

"Women are now employed in every sector of industry and business yet this fact is not reflected in the boardrooms of power."

I wish I could report differently, but in Canada and many countries around the world, representation of women in senior roles in organizations and in boardrooms of publicly traded companies is disproportionately low when considering the number of women who have the appropriate education, experience, and desire to justify their presence.

This disproportionate representation continues despite evidence that shows that when publicly traded companies have women in senior management roles, those organizations experience an average 47% increase of return on equity and a corresponding 55% increase of earnings.

It has been soundly shown that women want to lead at the highest levels: when 1,400 managers were asked if they had the desire to reach a top management position such as a C-suite role, 81% of men said YES, and 79% of women said YES.

Even with all the evidence before us for promoting women to senior roles, in Canada's 500 largest publicly traded corporations, 94% of the heads and 86% of the board positions are held by men.

Women hold only 5.8% of corporate executive positions and 14.5% of board positions.

So how do we reduce the gap between reality and aspiration? First we need to understand how history, biology, myth and media have shaped where we are today.

Secondly, we need to make different decisions if we truly want to create powerful women leaders.

1

THE GENDER WAGE GAP

The gender wage gap has a direct effect on the number of women leaders in a country. If you are not being paid well and in alignment with your peers, you have less income for advanced education, less income for at-home or institutional care for your children, less income for reliable transportation, and less income to network in environments where you could express your ideas and meet mentors.

The gender wage gap (GWG) represents the difference between the earnings of men and women. In Canada, the gap was measured in 2011 as a 12% difference between the earnings of men and women who are hourly workers (which often include unionized jobs). There was a 26% difference between male and female earnings for full-time, full-year earners. When annual earnings of male and females were compared (with no other criteria), there was a 31.5% gap between male and female earnings. These numbers mean that women make, on average, 68.5% of the income men do. This gap is even greater for women who are visible minorities, indigenous or have a disability.

Although the gender wage gap is caused by many factors, this book will focus primarily on those that affect leadership. Below we discuss our current situation regarding pay equality between men and women. In the following chapters we will look at how myth, media, and history of play have impacted women's participation in the workplace, as individuals and leaders.

Historical Inertia

The disparity in women's income can be traced not only to lack of recognition of women's economic worth, but government policy to reinforce that lack of recognition.

In the early part of the 20th century, governments and employers endorsed the concept of the family wage. This meant that a male worker would be paid enough to support a family. A woman would only be paid enough to support herself. The family wage led to setting women's salaries at about two-thirds of the male wage.

The reasoning at the time for the family wage was that working women would only be supporting themselves until marriage, which was of course the end goal to employment. Men, however, would be supporting a family. (There was no consideration given in this formula for situations where a woman's husband had died or was disabled, leaving his wife to financially support a family.)

We know that ideas change slowly and cultural beliefs even slower. In 1987 when I was working in a sales and marketing position in

Canada, I discovered that a fellow who was hired the week after I was and who had several years less experience than I, was hired for at a salary of $2,000 a year higher than mine. I asked my sales manager about it and he shrugged and said that the newer account representative "has a family, you know".

Although the manager probably wasn't instructed to pay me less, or the other employee more, the history of the wage gap continues to haunt us in unconscious bias.

Education Doesn't Guarantee Equal Pay

Women have been led to believe that if they match men in educational attainment, they will nullify the gender wage gap. To that end, we have seen 20% of all Canadian women complete an undergraduate university degree. Since 2002, women have earned 32-35% of all MBAs.

Based on Statistics Canada's 2011 National Household Survey, in the age group of 25-34, women hold more bachelor, medical, and master degrees than men. In the age 55-64 age group, women hold more than 45% of the bachelor and master's degrees.

Yet when we look at the education numbers, we can see that extra education only takes us so far in reducing the gender gap.

When women and men have:

- Less than a grade 9 high school education - women make **51.5%** of what the men make
- Some secondary school – women make **65.6%** of what the men make
- Graduated high school – women make **70.4%** of what the men make
- Some post-secondary education - women make **72.6%** of what the men make

- Post-secondary diploma - women make **71.6%** of what the men make
- University degree - women make **68.3%** of what the men make.

So we can see that as women gain more education, the wage gap narrows. But after a post-secondary diploma, women's wages stall and the gap starts to widen.

Occupational Segregation

It seems logical that jobs that are more dangerous, involve shiftwork or specific training should be better paid, yet this does not bare out statistically.

For example, compare a Licensed Practical Nurse (LPN) to a cable television service and maintenance technician (CTSMT).

LPN	2 years college	$10,500 tuition	$38,261
MTSMT	1-2 years on the job training	no personal financial commitment	$51,030

To become a LPN requires a two year college diploma and a personal financial commitment of $10,500 in tuition. To become a CTSMT requires one to two years of on the job training and no personal financial commitment. One would think that the LPN would make more money, considering the longer educational training, personal financial commitment, not to mention the shiftwork inherent in the position, and possible exposure to violent or infectious patients. However, the median earnings of the LPN is $38,261 and the CTSMT is $51,030. LPNs are 90% female and CTSMT are 97% male.

Although women work in every field, the job classes dominated by women tend to be paid less than those dominated by men. So, would it not make sense for women to enter male dominated fields to address this gender pay gap? Unfortunately, when job classes like telephone operators and bank tellers transitioned from being male dominated to female dominated job classes, the pay dropped overall.

The Caring Dilemma

In Canada today, 70% of mothers with children under the age of five work outside the home.

With the exception of the province of Quebec, approximately 40% of children in Canada between 0-5 years of age are cared for by parents and 25% are cared for in a licensed child care facility - leaving a gap of 35% to be cared in a variety of other ways (relatives, friends, unregulated child care facilities). Many parents have trouble finding a spot in a suitable child care facility. The economic impact on parents can be extremely high.

In Ontario, Canada, 94% of part-time workers who state that caring for children is the reason they didn't work full time are women.

Quebec, which has the most comprehensive provincial child care program for children ages 0-12, provides universal care for $7 a day, resulting in a rise in the female participation rate in their provincial work force from the lowest to the highest in Canada. This has resulted in moving children above the national average on standardized test scores and reducing the number of families experiencing poverty by 50%.

Women continue to usually be the parent in a double income family who takes the day off if a child is sick or the mother-in-law is in for day surgery. Single parent families (of which the majority are led by women) have little choice as to who that parent will be when a child is sick.

2

THE SPORTS WE PLAY MATTER

With the exception of the Toronto Blue Jays playing in the World Series of baseball and the Saskatchewan Roughriders making it to the Grey Cup of Canadian football, I don't watch team sports. Even as a girl in middle and high school, I didn't engage in team sports.

As I child, I played traditional games with other young girls and kick-the-can with neighborhood kids, but playing hockey, football or soccer was unheard of for girls in my age group. In high school in the late 1970s, there were fewer team sports for girls than there are today and I, like my peers, were shaped both by what we played and the rules of girl play.

If I were raising a daughter today, I would encourage her to play team sports - or at least to understand the psychology of team sport – because team sport rules are the rules of the workplace as much as the soccer field.

In the workplace, the players are older and less physically fit. The fields of play are boardrooms, not football fields. But team sport rules still determine the play. We may think that sport is only a metaphor for the relationships within the workplace, but the rules of sport directly affect success in the workplace.

Unfortunately, the rules of team sport that play out in the workplace are in direct contradiction to how most women (especially women over 40) think they need to communicate and behave to be hired, and promoted. Many women who are younger have had the advantage of understanding team sport because they had opportunities to play hockey, football and soccer - particularly at competitive levels. Women in my age group were more likely to date a jock than to be one.

So how can we make team sport rules work for us in the workplace? First, we need to accept that these rules exist and second, we need to understand the rules so we can utilize similar strategies. In this chapter, we will explore the rules of the game that impact success in the workplace.

Rule #1 - You'll Always Have A Coach

The idea that you will have a coach makes absolute sense when referring to sports - of course there is a coach! Sometimes a team has even more than one. When young men are raised in a sport environment, they enter the workplace expecting a coach to be present and willing to offer guidance. If there isn't one obviously available, they find one.

These mentors tell them who they should or should not share confidential information with, how to fast track their career to partner or senior manager, and explain the culture of the organization and team. Young men not only expect advice and influence, they use it. The advice could come from a superior, someone else in the organization who believes in them and wants to see them succeed, or an outsider who understands the culture and influencers of the particular field of endeavour.

Women have been aware of this network in the workplace for a long time and dubbed it the 'old boys club'. We saw it with men mentoring their friends' sons, the close camaraderie of men from the same schools or universities and with the symbolic 'iron' ring of Canadian engineering graduates. In past decades, women have tried to change or enter into the informal mentoring relationships that flourished within the 'old boys club', but it continued to perpetuate itself as a men's only arena to the exclusion women.

So women began to look to other women as mentors and started their own old girls club, with some challenges.

Throughout the thirty years I have been involved with women's groups, women have put an increasing emphasis on the value of women mentoring and developing formal and informal mentoring relationships with other women. Unfortunately, the initial success of these mentoring relationships was limited for two reasons. Often there are too few women in places of influence, power or success that have time to mentor younger women on their way up the ladder. Secondly, younger women expect a balancing out of relationship. The one-sidedness of mentoring made many women uncomfortable in accepting help or advice, feeling that there should be a give and take or reciprocal effect to the relationship.

Not unlike breakfast clubs across the country where business men meet, socialize and aggressively support each other's businesses, women began to build their own networks. Some female networks were successful and others were not. Unlike men in male-only networks, some women in female-only networks felt that the other members only wanted to sell them their service or product and weren't concerned about them as a person or about supporting their goals. Some networks became more social than business related or ceased to function altogether. This inability for female networks - formed for the sole purpose of career and business development - to cement, may have to do with the belief that some women possess about relationship equality. Give and take must be present. If the relationship is one-sided and one participant gains more than the other, something is wrong.

So what about men mentoring women?

Women are equally challenged by developing mentoring relationships with men as mentors, but for different reasons. It is sometimes difficult for women to be comfortable with the idea of being mentored by a man, even though there is a much greater supply of men in senior leadership positions than women.

One concern both men and women have in regards to male-female mentoring relationships is the innate social nature of connection. With a male mentor and female mentee (or vice versa), advice may be misinterpreted to be other than useful information and guidance. In today's litigious world, many men are cautious about being personal with a woman in the workplace. Yet - a mentoring relationship by definition is personal - the mentor takes the mentee's success personally.

When we look at the close relationships within a male network, we see people taking each other's success personally. They are like a group of players and coaches - just filling each other in on the most important plays and where extra practice and skill development is required.

As women, we need to understand it is permissible to receive without giving and to develop relationships that are not based on friendship, but on our own best interest.

Rule #2 - Try Out

Men - and women who have played team sport - know that you don't have to be the best player to try out for the position. You have to merely have desire and a degree of knowledge or skill. That's what trying out means. In the workplace, this rule plays out in knowing that it is not necessary to totally understand a job to apply for it. There will be a coach there to help us learn the new job or task.

Women often look at a job posting and say "I'm not sure if I'm really qualified." The beauty of a tryout perspective is it gives the person a "What the hell, I might as well give it a shot" attitude that works to their advantage in the workplace. This attitude can be advantageous whether we are interviewing for a job, asking for a promotion, or even suggesting we get the windowed office or the closest parking spot. An attitude of "Nothing ventured, nothing gained" moves us forward into positions where we can learn as we go. We can't win the race, if we don't even enter. We can't score, if we don't shoot. (Even describing the act of initiation often takes on sports metaphor.)

On top of the advantage that men have in the 'give it a try' attitude they learned with team sport, their physiology also gives them an advantage over women. As children, boys enjoy taking risks. Most boys are impressed by other boys who take risks, especially if the risk-taker succeeds. Girls are less likely to enjoy risk-taking for its own sake and are much less likely to be impressed by risk-taking behaviour in others. According to researcher, Leonard Sax, girls may be willing to take risks, but they are less likely to seek out risky situations just for the sake of living dangerously.

Part of this difference is that risky and dangerous activities trigger a flight-or-fight response that gives a tingly charge, an excitement that many boys find irresistible. The increased heart rate, dilated pupils, a surge of adrenaline in the blood preparing them to fight or run away is how men physiologically respond to risky situations.

Women, however, respond to threat and confrontation with a 'the puke-and-pee' response; they feel dizzy, nauseous, and need to go to the bathroom frequently. As little individual study has been done on how women specifically respond to threat and stressful situations, we see again that much scientific data is based on male studies extrapolated to include women.

The assertive male risk-taking strategy sometimes works for men and sometimes leads them to over-estimate their ability. For example, nearly all drowning victims are male. According to research by the American Journal of Public Health, men consistently overestimate their ability to swim in threatening situations.

Women consistently underestimate their ability and minimize their risk of failure. In her book, *Women Don't Ask: Negotiation and the Gender Divide*, Linda Babcock studied students graduating from Carnegie Mellon University with a master's degree in a business related field. She found that the starting salaries of the men were about 8% on average higher than those of the women. The men were paid about $4,000 more per year.

Babcock looked to see who asked for more money during the job finding process. Only 7% of the female students had asked compared with 57% of the male students. Students who asked for more money received a starting salary that was $4,053 higher on average than those who did not ask. The male students were more inclined to take the risk of offending the hiring human resource officer for the sake of a higher starting salary

On an hourly rate comparison of employed Canadians, women make an average of 12% less than men and in areas of full time/full year employment, women make on average 26% less than men. In a Statistics Canada National Graduate Survey, the graduates from year 2000 show that two years later in 2002, the median salary for the female university grads working full time was $37,000 and for men it was $42,000.

Although women's cautious risk-taking strategy mentioned above can justify some of the difference in the gender gap, there are many other factors holding back women's success. But certainly having a 'give it a try' attitude can move us forward in job attainment, promotion and income increase.

Rule #3 - There's Only One Quarterback

The unwritten rule of quarterbacks and captains is that there is only one on the field at a time - often only one on the team at a time. There is one leader and you are the leader or you are not. If you want to be the leader, you must remove the leader from their position of power. This one-up/one-down theory means that there is only one leader at a time - and you lead, you follow or you get benched. You are either up in leadership position or down in follow position.

As I think of my childhood and the games I played with my sisters and female friends, I reflect that leadership was not about competition, hierarchy or role restriction. Change of leadership was not due to an ousting of the current leader or an assignment by an outside coach. You became the leader simply because it was your turn next.

Competition was not about taking a risk, but rather you won by not making a mistake. In musical chairs, you won by not being left standing when all the other players had found a spot. A good strategy was to stay close to a chair and not risk going too far away from your safe bet. In jump rope, when it is your turn, you jump and your friends turn the rope until – you make a mistake. And then you lose.

This means in the workplace, some women expect there to be dire consequences if a mistake is made. This makes women overly cautious about trying new things and overly careful regarding details.

Another effect of this unwritten rule is that women expect promotion when they have been there the longest, or when they have worked hard or without error. They think if they are patient, all good things will come to them. The meek may indeed inherit the earth, however without a 'tryout' attitude; they won't be inheriting the workplace.

Rule #4 - Shake the Winner's Hand

The purpose of shaking the winner's or loser's hand at the end of the game or match is to prove that the players were competitive at the time of the game but now that it is over, they can be civilized and friendly. It reinforces the opportunity for the losers to save face in the moment of defeat. You are a poor loser if you don't shake hands and a poor winner if you gloat over your victory.

This rule is one of the more confusing ones for women because it seems that those who follow this rule are incongruent and insincere. "How can you argue with me in the boardroom, criticize my proposal, even demote me and then expect me to go for drinks after work. Screw you!"

By not separating 'work' out as a game, women are often accused of taking things personally when they are disagreed with or receive negative feedback. Women may also find it difficult to work with people they do not like or continue to work with someone with whom they have had a disagreement. This is seen by others as not being a team player or being unwilling to put personal feelings aside for the betterment of the whole.

The sports metaphors discussed above are still in force in many organizations. As we slowly move to gender balanced leadership teams, new managers - many of them women and many of them aware of team sports rules - may change the way we see these issues. The purpose of this discussion is not whether we can change the way it is – the purpose is for women to understand that some workplaces play under team sport rules. By understanding the rules, we can win the game.

3

DISNEY
AND THE POWER OF PRINCESS

We develop many of our beliefs about ourselves and the world when we are children. Parents, educators, religious figures and media all influence our beliefs. The four generations – Traditionalists, Boomers, Generation X and Generation Y – who work in our organizations today have been shaped by these four influencers, with religion playing a diminishing role with each generation and media playing an increasing one. The influence of media through television and movies has shaped our worldview and our perspectives on gender.

In the following chapters, we will examine the impact of the iconic fairy tales presented as animated movies by the Disney system: Cinderella, Sleeping Beauty, Snow White and Beauty and the Beast, and

the 'sequels' they have spawned. These four animated movies, as created by Disney, deliver strong negative messages regarding realistic body image, assertiveness, independence, initiative, and the pursuit of knowledge. In addition, this negative effect is compounded by the ability of children to see these movies and hear the films' songs over and over again, thanks to DVD technology.

Many of us have fond memories of the first time we saw these movies and don't necessarily understand the consequences of longing to be the princess. Nor do we necessarily detect how all four 'stories' continue to be reincarnated again and again for our viewing pleasure and our belief system's shaping, even as adults.

Following the next chapters, we will discuss how the impact of Disney has, contrary to popular belief, increased its influence over women to choose passivity over action and sadness over happiness.

4

CINDERELLA
THERE WILL ALWAYS BE A
FAIRY GODMOTHER

New edition, Old Story

The voluminous skirt of Cinderella's dress led the way as she moved forward. Her pale skin was frosted with glitter and her hair was a brilliant gold. Her hands settled briefly on her tiny waist. "I don't really have organs anymore", joked the 24 year old actress. "Everything is squeezed in and then pushed down. I can only eat soup, no real food", she whispered, as if even her voice had been squished into submission. The corset cinched her waist to 21 inches, and eating food was impossible. Merely breathing was challenging.

Lily James starred as Cinderella in the 2015 movie of the same name. It is a live action Disney remake of the studio's 1950 American animated musical fantasy film. The 1950 animated film was based on the fairy tale, *Cendrillon*, by Charles Perrault. The 2015 film was based on the 1950 film, *Cinderella*, and stars Cate Blanchett as the stepmother Lady Tremaine and Helena Bonham Carter as Cinderella's Fairy Godmother.

Cinderella is the most common Disney princess (both in the original story and reincarnation) and her influence is reflected in women's beliefs about themselves, money, relationships and work. She is the heroine of a plot that captures the fantasy of youth. Cinderella is a pretty, spunky girl controlled by a wicked stepmother and evil stepsisters. The man who is going to take her away from all of this is a prince who is rich, handsome and charming.

Although the need for the prince is not as strong in this new film, the message to viewers is more developed in the area of passivity and inaction. Cinderella is told, and tells the audience, that if you "have courage, be kind, all will be well." Courage and kindness are certainly good traits to develop, but inaction - not so much. The film's Ella is good and kind to the point of passivity. She does not step up, speak up or put herself forward in any way. She expects that all that is required is to be kind and the universe will deal with injustices and deliver her wants and needs.

The Animated Version - Disney

Ella is the cherished only child of a widowed aristocrat. Concerned about his daughter having no mothering influence and desirous perhaps of companionship himself, her father marries Lady Tremaine. His new wife has two daughters from a previous marriage (Drizella and Anastasia) who he hopes will become true sisters to his only daughter.

Alas Ella's stepmother is a cold and cruel woman and when Ella's father dies unexpectedly, the stepmother begins a campaign to demoralize Ella, including encouraging mistreatment of the girl by her own daughters, Drizella and Anastasia. On the death of her husband, Lady Tremaine takes over the management of the estate, but does it poorly, and eventually drives the family's finances into ruin. As domestic staff are let go one by one, Ella is instructed to take over minor duties of housekeeping. Eventually all the domestic staff are fired, leaving Ella as the only servant in the house. The favoured daughter has become a kitchen servant in her own home. As she spends more and more time in the kitchen, close to the fire and ashes, Ella's stepsisters begin to call her Cinder Ella.

In spite of her treatment at the hands of her stepfamily, Cinderella grows up to be a loving and caring young woman, her concern even extending to barnyard animals and the mice and birds that often invade the mansion. (This ability to speak to and understand animal conversations is a common trait of Disney princesses).

Unknown to Ella in her stifling world of domestic drudgery, at the nearby palace, the King and Grand Duke decide to throw a ball for the Prince, in hopes of getting him married off so their line of monarchs would continue to reign. The King invites all the eligible maidens in the land to the ball and an invitation arrives at the home of Cinderella.

Cinderella asks her stepmother if she too can go to the ball, as the invitation stipulates every eligible maiden may attend. Lady Tremaine agrees, on the condition that Cinderella finishes her chores and finds an appropriate dress to wear.

Cinderella finds no time to complete an ensemble for herself, but her furry friends step in to assist, fixing a gown previously owned by Cinderella's mother and modifying the design with beads and a sash discarded by her stepsisters. (Not only can birds and mice communicate with Cinderella, they can sew as well).

However, when Cinderella comes down wearing her new dress, Lady Tremaine compliments the gown and points out the modifications to her daughters, knowing that they would not leave the dress in one piece. The two stepsisters rip off the sash and beads, destroying the gown.

Cinderella watches from the window as the carriage takes her stepfamily off to the ball. She runs to the garden and cries about her misfortune and missed opportunities.

From nowhere appears, magically of course, a fairy godmother. With a flick of her magic wand, the fairy godmother transforms a pumpkin into a carriage, mice into horses, Cinderella's horse into a coachman, and a dog into a footman.

The fairy godmother waves her magic wand once more and Cinderella is no longer barefoot and dressed in a torn, outdated dress but is garbed in an opulent satin ball gown and matching glass slippers.

The fairy godmother helps Cinderella into the coach, telling her to be certain to return by twelve for the spell ends at the stroke of midnight.

At the ball, the Prince rejects every girl until he sees Cinderella. She dazzles the prince with her beauty and they dance together most of the evening. (This must have been quite a feat considering she was wearing inflexible shoes of glass.) The other guests whisper to each other, wondering who the beautiful stranger is.

Cinderella and the Prince fall in love, while walking through the gardens and dancing alone throughout the castle grounds. When the clock starts to chime midnight, Cinderella flees from the Prince and runs to her coach. On the way down the stairs to her soon-to-become-pumpkin conveyance, she accidentally loses one of her glass slippers. Anxious not to be caught in the middle of the spell, she leaves the slipper behind and hastens away.

On the way home, the spell reverses and Cinderella is left with four mice, a dog, a horse and a pumpkin - and one glass slipper (faulty magic).

Meanwhile, back at the castle, the prince discovers the slipper and becomes determined to find the girl that it fits and marry her. Urged by his son, early the next morning, the King proclaims that the Grand Duke will visit every house in the kingdom to find the girl whose foot fits the glass slipper.

When news reaches Cinderella's household, her stepmother and her two stepsisters prepare for the Duke's arrival. When Lady Tremaine hears Cinderella humming a song from the ball the evening before, she realizes that her stepdaughter was the girl the Prince had danced with and whose foot would fit the glass slipper. She locks Cinderella in the attic, determined that one of her daughters may yet be princess to the kingdom's prince.

Luckily, once again due to magic and the uncanny ability of animals and Disney princesses to converse, the barnyard animals and house mice rescue Cinderella in time to catch the departing Duke. Her stepsisters have tried to shove their large feet into the glass slipper with no success. Lady Tremaine knows that the slipper will fit her stepdaughter but is determined that Cinderella will not succeed where her daughters have failed and trips the servant carrying the slipper. He drops the glass slipper and it smashes on the floor. Not to be outdone, Cinderella quietly produces the other glass slipper from the pocket of her apron. A happy Duke slides the slipper onto her foot, and it fits perfectly.

Cinderella and the Prince celebrate their wedding and live happily ever after.

The Original Story – Cinder Cat

Cinderella was first recorded by the Italian writer, Giambattista Basile in his books of fairy tales *Lo cunto de li cunti overo lo trattenemiento de peccerille* or *The Tale of Tales* and *Entertainment for Little Ones*. His tales were published by his sister in 1634 and 1636 after his death, under the pseudonym, Gian Alesio Abbatutis.

Although neglected for some time, Basile's work received considerable attention after the Brothers Grimm praised it highly as the first national collection of fairy tales. Basile's tale of Cinderella is considered the earliest version.

Basile tells the tale as this:

Little Zezolla was no victim of circumstance. Her mother was dead and her father had remarried. Zezolla isn't too happy about her father's new relationship and dislikes his new wife, so she plots against her stepmother, with the assistance of her nanny. Together, they manage to kill the stepmother by slamming the lid of a heavy chest on her neck. (So much for the innocent victim who is cheerful in spite of her lot in life!)

Zezolla encourages her father to remarry - with the chosen wife to be her co-conspiring, murdering nanny. Zezolla then becomes a victim herself when the nanny brings her six daughters to live with them. Shortly after Zezolla' s father's death, the murdering Zezolla is given the chore of cleaning the grate and gets the nickname, Cinder Cat from her six stepsisters.

Cinder Cat finds a magic date tree. From a date, pops out a fairy that can grant her a wish. She asks the fairy to dress her in glorious clothes. Garbed as an aristocrat, Cinder Cat begins to attend a round of parties and balls frequented by the peers of the realm. At the very first event, she meets the King and his entourage. The King is intrigued by the mysterious young woman.

At each event, the King falls more and more in love with Cinder Cat, even though, or perhaps because, she is coy about her name and where she resides. Unable to determine her identity and unwilling to wait for her to disclose the information, he finally sends out a servant to follow her home from a party, but she eludes the servant and disappears into the night.

At the next ball, the determined servant of the King visually tracks Zezolla around the dance floor and follows her from a ball, leaving at the precise time when she departs, clinging haphazardly to the back of her carriage. When the coachman increases speed, the servant falls off. And so does Zezolla's slipper - or as much of a slipper as was worn in the 1600s.

(In those times, shoes were covered by a high heeled overshoe so that the woman's dress was not damaged by mud or other unspeakable things that were present on streets in the 1600s. The overshoe was several inches high, probably made of leather and protected the wearer's dance shoe.)

The servant returns to the King with no further knowledge of Cinder Cat's identity.

The King throws a party for the women in the kingdom. Zezolla cannot turn down a party and attends. When the King begins to try the overshoe on each woman, Zezolla admits that it belongs to her. The King and Cinder Cat marry – and of course live happily ever after.

The Modern Version - Pretty Woman

Pretty Woman is a 1990 American romantic comedy film starring Richard Gere and Julia Roberts. Its story centers on down-on-her-luck Hollywood call girl Vivian Ward, who is hired by Edward Lewis, a wealthy businessman, to be his escort for several business and social functions, and their developing relationship over the course of her week-long stay with him. Like many princess movies, it became one of the highest money makers of its year and one of the most popular films of all time.

Edward Lewis (Gere), a successful workaholic businessman and corporate raider in Los Angeles on business, accidentally takes a detour on Hollywood Boulevard while looking for Beverly Hills. He encounters a call girl named Vivian Ward (Roberts), who mistakes him for a possible client. He only wants directions so makes a deal with her to pay her if she shows him the way to his destination. Intrigued by her knowledge and wit (and ability to drive a stick shift), he hires her to

spend the night with him, treating her to strawberries and champagne.

The morning after, Edward hires Vivian to stay with him for a week as an escort for social events. She advises him that it will cost him, and he agrees to pay her $3,000 and gives her money and access to his credit cards to buy suitable elegant clothing. (Tall, dark, handsome and rich as all Disney princes are, Richard Gere's character has become the prince to Julia Roberts's Vivian).

That evening is an important dinner for the prince (he's buying and pillaging companies as a corporate raider) and he instructs his princess to go and buy an appropriate dress for dinner.

Alas for poor Vivian, she goes shopping on Rodeo Drive and none of the shopkeepers will give her the time of day (dressed up as she is in thigh-high boots and a leather miniskirt). She returns to the hotel and finds her fairy godmother (actually godfather) in the guise of the hotel manager, played by Hector Elizondo. He sends her to an exclusive shop for women who are moving up in her line of work.

Later he gives her lessons on dining etiquette so she won't embarrass herself or her prince at dinner.

The prince finds her waiting for him in the hotel lounge, dressed in a short black cocktail dress, her makeup subtle and soft, her hair styled in long, luxurious curls. He begins falling in love with her.

The rest of the movie is about her assisting him in understanding his corporate raider personality and his real desire to build businesses, not destroy them. However, as he moves to a more enlightened direction for his life, his co-worker sees his own business interests deteriorating. The prince's colleague blames Vivian and attacks her. Richard Gere's character saves the day by punching out his business associate.

Edward asks her if she will be his mistress (live in a great apartment with a healthy allowance) but she says she wants the whole fairy tale and they go their separate ways. He quickly realizes that he cannot live without her and seeks her out, with the help of the limo driver who knows her address. She throws herself into his arms and (we assume) they marry and live happily ever after.

Another woman who became a princess at the hands of a wealthy, handsome prince.

The Old Version Revised – Ever After

The 1998 American romantic comedy drama, *Ever After: A Cinderella Story*, stars Drew Barrymore as the Cinderella character (Danielle) and Anjelica Huston as the stepmother. Although Barrymore plays a modern woman in a 1600s setting, the theme is similar to the traditional story: her father dies leaving her at the mercy of her evil stepmother and stepsisters, the stepmother systematically sells off everything of value, and the stepdaughter has been relegated to the class of servant.

In 17th-century France, widower Auguste de Barbarac, father of eight-year-old Danielle, marries a baroness with two young daughters, Maguerite and Jacqueline. He dies of a heart attack shortly after his marriage. His last words were of Danielle, which causes the Baroness to envy her stepdaughter and treat her miserably for the next ten years. Although Danielle's stepsister Jacqueline is kind to her, Marguerite is cruel and demeaning.

One day while collecting apples, Danielle sees a man stealing her father's horse and stops him with a well-pitched apple. Discovering the horse thief to be the local prince, the girl is paid off with a bag of gold in exchange for her silence. Danielle decides to use the money to rescue her servant who the Baroness had recently sold to pay off her debts. Knowing the servant would shortly sent to the Americas, Danielle dresses as a noblewoman and tries to buy back the servant but is refused until the prince overhears and orders the servant's release.

Intrigued by Danielle's mysterious identity, and amazed by her eloquence and passionate pleas, the prince begs for her name. Danielle gives Henry the name of her aristocratic mother who died giving birth to Danielle.

Through an unfortunate swimming encounter with Leonardo da Vinci who is in the King's employ, Danielle meets the prince again. He is intrigued by her intelligence and outspoken ways and calls on her at her home. Luckily (through forewarning and careful maneuvering), the visit did not come to the attention of Danielle's stepmother.

Over the next several days, Danielle and the prince come to know each other. She sparks his desire to achieve some meaning in his life and with her help he discovers his true purpose, immediately ceasing his life of boredom and discontent.

At this same time, the stepmother is putting pieces of the puzzle together and realizes that Danielle has been meeting the prince and using her dead mother's name. The Queen asks Danielle's stepmother if she knows anything about this new courtier. The stepmother replies that the courtier under discussion is living with them and is engaged to be married.

The Queen is saddened by this and tells the prince the bad news. Disheartened, he agrees to attend a ball to find a wife among the eligible women in the region.

The stepmother, by this time fully enlightened regarding the comings and goings of her stepdaughter, locks Danielle in the kitchen so she cannot go to the ball (a common theme here).

With the assistance of Leonardo da Vinci, (the godperson in this story), Danielle escapes the kitchen and co-creates a wonderful costume for the ball. She is whisked to the palace in Leonardo's carriage and arrives with the traditional grand entrance.

As the prince meets Danielle and leads her into the ball, her stepmother steps forth and exposes her as a servant in her household. The prince, with classist disgust at her station in life, turns his back on Danielle and she runs away.

Leonardo chastises the prince for being shallow and not appreciating Danielle's fine assets and accomplishments. By the time the prince realizes he cannot live without Danielle, she has been sold by her stepmother to an evil man who has leg-chained her to prevent her escape.

As soon as an opportunity arises, Danielle uses her fine abilities with a sword and dagger to bring the despicable fellow to his knees, unlocking her chains and setting herself free. As she leaves her captor's home, the prince rides into the courtyard to save her life (a little too late, I would say).

He begs for her forgiveness and she forgives him. They are married, live happily ever after - and throw her evil stepmother and stepsister Marguerite into the servant ranks as a bedclothes laundry person.

Moral to the Story

There have been over 700 versions of the Cinderella tale, told over 2,500 years to millions of children.

When we look at the common themes of the stories about Cinderella, the strongest element is the fairy godmother character. In Basile's Cinder-Cat, it was a date tree fairy. In the Disney's animated version as well as the recent live-action edition, it was a bibbity-bobbity-boo fairy godmother. In *Pretty Woman*, it was the hotel manager who knew the way of the world and felt sorry for the princess-to-be. In *Ever After*, Leonardo da Vinci was the magic element. In all examples, the magic allowed for construction of a costume.

Does this teach us that women need intervention of others to get what we want or wish for in life? Do we need others to step in and bridge us from where we are in our lives to where we want to ideally be - without any of the effort or learning in the middle that are so necessary for growth and personal development?

The problem with wishing for fairy godmothers is that we don't set reachable goals for ourselves or take the determined steps towards making those goals come true. It is fine to wish for things. What is important is to take responsibility for turning those wishes into goals and goals into achievements.

In a society where instant success is seen as a true possibility - whether it is a lottery ticket or creating a YouTube channel where you rake in advertising dollars sharing your shopping opinions – the lure of magic is compelling. Although we may not think fairy godmothers are true, perhaps we still think that by some magic force the perfect man may still come into our lives and fulfill all our wants and needs. Or we will be discovered in some way and we will become famous.

I am sure many of us dream about what we would do with a big lottery win. If we won two million dollars, we wouldn't have to work so hard, or work at all. The instant gratification of lottery winnings and fairy godmothers can be very compelling.

Not only could a fairy godmother make our dreams come true, without her or some other form of magic, we are doormats for the play of life. Without a fairy godmother, we cannot achieve or succeed. But if I had a fairy godmother, I could have anything I wanted. Belief in the fairy godmother stops us from taking action in our lives because we feel we can't really succeed without the magic.

The underlying theme of victimization in this and other fairy tales reinforces our belief that women can't take care of themselves - can't achieve their own dreams and goals. It also tells us that we should expect to be mistreated, but that being a victim always pays off.

We need to be our own fairy godmother and make our own dreams come true.

5

SLEEPING BEAUTY
ONE DAY MY PRINCE WILL COME

The Disney Version

As I remember it from my childhood, watching the Disney animated film of the same name, Sleeping Beauty was a tale of a beautiful young princess who pricks her finger on the tip of a spindle (a stick that has a notch in the top, used to draw out natural fibres for spinning into thread, and a long narrow body around which the thread is wound when spun) and falls immediately into a dark and dreamless sleep for 100 years.

This 1959 American musical fantasy film was based on The Sleeping Beauty interpretation by Charles Perrault and the tale Little Briar Rose by The Brothers Grimm.

King Stefan and Queen Leah welcome the birth of their daughter, the Princess Aurora by proclaiming a holiday for their subjects to pay honour to the princess and celebrate her birth. At the gathering for her christening she is betrothed to Prince Phillip, the young and only son of King Hubert so that their kingdoms will be united.

Among the guests are two 'good' fairies called Flora and Fauna who give the child the gifts of beauty and song. A dark and evil fairy named Maleficent appears (making quite an entrance). Maleficent curses the princess, proclaiming that Aurora will grow in grace and beauty, but before the sun sets on her 16th birthday, she will prick her finger on the spindle of a spinning wheel and die. After Maleficent departs, a third 'good' witch, Merryweather uses her blessing to change Maleficient's curse so Aurora will fall into a very deep sleep instead of dying. A sleep that can only be disturbed by true love's first kiss. Taking a proactive measure, King Stefan orders all spinning wheels in the kingdom to be burned.

The fairies take further action and remove the baby from the castle to a woodcutter's cottage in the forest where they plan to watch over her until the day of her 16th. (Both the actions by the fairies and the King seem illogical. If the child is safe until her 16th birthday, it would have made sense to burn all the spindles and spirit her away shortly before her 16th birthday, instead of bringing her home on the day of her projected fate).

The fairies give Aurora a new name for protection - Briar Rose – and she grows into a beautiful young woman (as all Disney princesses do). On the day of her 16th birthday, the three fairies ask Rose to gather berries in the forest so they can prepare a birthday party for her. While singing in the forest, Rose attracts the attention of Prince Phillip, now a handsome young man (as all Disney princes are). The two fall instantly in love, unaware of having been betrothed when they were only babies Rose asks Phillip to come to her cottage that evening to meet the fairies that protect her.

But alas this true love will have a rocky path. When Aurora arrives home the fairies tell her the truth about her parents and that she is betrothed to a prince and therefore cannot see the man she has just met again. Meanwhile, Phillip tells his father of the peasant girl he met in the forest and of course his father convinces him to never see her again. There is much gnashing of teeth and tumbling of tears.

That evening, the fairies take Aurora back to the castle. Maleficent appears and lures Aurora away from the fairies. She tricks the princess into touching an enchanted spinning wheel and Aurora pricks her finger, falling into a death-like sleep.

The good fairies place Aurora on a bed in the highest tower and place a powerful spell on all the people in the kingdom, causing them to fall in a deep sleep until the spell on their princess is broken.

The prince discovers that Briar Rose is his fiancée and becomes determined to save her. Maleficent attempts to keep the prince away from the princess, using all of her magic talents including magic thorns and a fire-breathing dragon against him. But the prince has good magic on his side and soon overcomes all the challenges.

Sleeping Beauty lay on a bed high in the castle while magically everything else in the castle was frozen with medieval sci-fi magic. She was awakened by the kiss of her handsome prince - exactly as was

foretold by the good fairies that mitigated the initial death spell. The castle sprang to life, including the people (with minimal muscle cramping).

The princess and prince, of course, marry and live happily ever after.

The Original Story by Basile

Sleeping Beauty is a tale originally from Italy and was first written down in 1636 by Giambattista Basile in his 1634 work, *The Pentamerone*. He called the tale *"Sun, Moon and Talia"*. In 1697, it was recorded by Frenchman, Charles Perrault and first titled *"The Sleeping Beauty."*

Basile's tale went like this:

There was the traditional horrid curse at her birth, not by a witch or evil fairy, but by her father's astrologer. Instead of dying of the prick of a spinning wheel, her life would cease due to a poisoned splinter of flax.

Although the girl, Talia, wasn't the daughter of a king (merely the daughter of a lord), her father was still a powerful and wealthy man and just like the outlawing of spinning wheels in the Perrault and Disney version, flax was forbidden anywhere near the little girl.

The curse of the stars was stronger than the power of the lord and one day the young woman, Talia, sees an old woman spinning flax on a spindle. She asks the woman if she can stretch the flax herself, but as soon as she begins to spin, a splinter of flax goes under her fingernail, and she drops to the ground, apparently dead.

Unable to stand the thought of burying his child, the lord takes Talia to one of his country estates. Bereft of his daughter's love, he places her on a velvet throne, covers her with lace, locks the front door and never returns.

One day, a king (as opposed to a prince in the newer version) is hunting in the nearby forest and his falcon flies into the lord's empty house. The King, following the falcon, enters the house through a window and discovers the sleeping Talia. He tries to wake her, first with soft words and then with shouts, but to no avail. Then, as any all-powerful king of the day might do, he carries her to the bed and rapes her. Afterwards, he returns home to his wife and children and promptly forgets about the sleeping beauty. (This would be really disgusting if he thought she was dead, but he thought she was only sleeping - and therefore his behaviour might be only termed disgraceful, scandalous and totally lacking in chivalry.)

Nine months after the rape, the sleeping beauty gives birth to twins, one of which in its enthusiasm for mother's milk starts to suck on her finger. This action removes the flax splinter and the young woman finds herself on a bed with two squalling infants and a mess to clean up. To say the least - she was surprised.

She names them Sun and Moon and lives with them in the house.

Just as she has things under control thanks to the help of some fairies that magically appeared, the erstwhile lover remembers his fond excursion into the forest near her home and returns. When he finds his unconscious lover awake and mother of his children, he says he's overjoyed. I'm a bit sceptical - how many men do you know are excited when they produce children from a one night stand? After several days, he leaves, promising (have we heard this one before?) to one day return for her and the children.

Unfortunately, the King talks in his sleep and soon the Queen catches on to the true nature of his 'hunting activities'. He had never mentioned Talia and the twins to the Queen, but she is suspicious and forces the King's secretary to tell her everything. She forges an invitation in the King's name asking Talia to bring Sun and Moon to his court.

When Talia and family arrive, the King is not there. The Queen orders the cook to cut up and cook the children for supper for the King and throws Talia in the dungeon.

At dinner, the King compliments his wife on the wonderful meal preparations and the Queen mumbles "they're yours, all yours". Little did she know, but the cook had hid the children and cooked a pair of lambs instead.

Early the next morning, the King departs on a trip. As soon as he has left, the Queen calls forth Talia from the dungeon. She screams at Talia "So you're the bitch who is causing me such pain!" (Talk about violence and bad language in these early fairy tales!) Talia replies that it was not her fault, that the King had his way with her while she was unconscious. The Queen does not believe her and instructs her men to throw Talia into the bonfire.

Talia, desperate to buy time, asks the Queen to let her remove her clothes so that at least something remains of who she is. After each piece of clothing, Talia screams, hoping that the King will return in time. Finally, she is naked and the men drag her to the bonfire.

Suddenly (or should I say finally as Basile was leaving the saving the beautiful girl to the very last moment it seemed), the King returns and demands to know what is happening. His wife tells him that Talia would be burned and that he had unknowingly eaten his own children. The King commands that his wife, his secretary, and the cook be thrown into the fire instead.

Luckily for the cook, he did not cook Sun and Moon but left them in his wife's safekeeping. As soon as the children are brought to the kind, the cook's death sentence is revoked.

The King and Talia marry and live happily ever after. (The cook is rewarded with the title of Royal Chamberlain.)

Moral of the story

This fairy tale preaches the lesson of the value of safekeeping your virtue, which would have been the concern of most parents at the time. Although Talia's king (prince) did finally show up, we don't know for certain what would have happened if she and the children had not been brought to his court by the Queen. What if the King had never sent for her? She could have ended up as just one more single mother statistic.

Fairy tales develop over time based on the desire of the storyteller to instill a certain lesson or moral in the listener. The story of Sleeping Beauty in its modern version tries to teach us that as women, we are out of control to save ourselves and we will - even though forewarned - put ourselves in positions of danger where we will need a prince to rescue us.

It is easy to dismiss this story as exactly what it is - a fairy tale. But, researchers have found that by the age of seven or so, we have created a large portion of our beliefs and attitudes about life and how we should function in the world. (In fact, we spend the next seventy years getting over the negative beliefs we developed in the first seven!)

Have you met women whose fairy tale might have played out like the first part of this story? Where the prince came, stayed briefly - and then left the woman with a mess to clean up?

Have you delayed doing or experiencing something exciting, waiting for your prince to enter your life? Have you put off travelling to a certain place in the world, just in case you go there on your honeymoon? Have you postponed buying a house or other property, in case you need something bigger if you get married soon? Are you waiting until you have gained your spouse or boyfriend's approval to begin an educational program or start an entrepreneurial endeavour? Did you choose a career that does not require education or skills because it was "just until I get married"?

Consider:

- In the UK in 2014, there were 1.8 million lone mothers with dependent children (dependent meaning that they are either under 16, or aged 16 to 18 and in full-time education).
- In Canada in 2014, there were 1.82 million widowed people: 384,210 men and 1,435,040 women.
- In Canada in 2015: 1,159,950 men reported their marital status as divorced and 1,402,800 women did as well.

It is clear that women are more likely to be divorced, widowed or single parents than men are. A high proportion of women are not living the life of a traditional wife and mother. Although we may want the fairy tale princess story of one day having a tall, handsome, wealthy man to sweep us off our feet so will never be concerned about single dances or bills again – the reality is different for many women.

Can any of us afford the luxury of the "it's just until I get married" attitude? Women have been and are today in the workforce for economic reasons. The few women who have the luxury of not having to earn an income are fewer than ever before.

We never know if and when we might be solely responsible for the economic wellbeing of ourselves and our families. Even if marriage and children never enter the picture, should we live a 'waiting life'? I think we deserve better, don't you

6

SNOW WHITE
BEAUTY CAN BE DANGEROUS

The Disney Version

Roy and Walt Disney released the film, *Snow White and the Seven Dwarfs*, in 1937. An American animated musical fantasy film, the story was based on the German fairy tale by the Brothers Grimm and was the first full-length film in what has come to be called the Walt Disney Animated Classics series.

Once upon a time, in a land far, far away, there lived a beautiful princess called Snow White. The princess lived with her stepmother, a vain and wicked Queen with magical powers. The Queen feared that Snow White's beauty may one day surpass her own and every day asked her magic mirror, "Magic Mirror on the wall - who is the fairest of us all?"

The mirror would always reply, "You, O Queen, are fairest of all."

But one day, when Snow White's beauty surpassed the beauty of her stepmother, the Queen's magic mirror replied to her daily question, "Thou art fair, O Queen, tis true, but Snow White is fairer than you."

The jealous Queen was furious and called for her huntsman. She instructed him to take Snow White into the forest, kill her and bring back her heart as evidence.

The next day, Snow White and the huntsman entered the forest. Stricken by her beauty (or by his conscience), he finds he cannot fulfill his task. He tells her of the Queen's agenda and instructs her to run deep into the forest.

A frightened Snow White wanders in the forest through the night and in the morning she is befriended by woodland creatures who guide her to a cottage in a clearing. She knocks on the door, but there is no answer. She opens the door and enters. Inside the house, there were seven of everything: seven chairs, seven beds, seven plates. Snow White assumes the cottage is the untidy home of seven orphaned children and begins to straighten and clean.

But in reality (as much reality exists in a Disney cartoon), the cottage belongs to Doc, Grumpy, Happy, Sleepy, Bashful, Sneezy, Dopey - seven adult dwarfs who work in a nearby mine. Returning home, they are alarmed to find their cottage clean and suspect that an intruder has invaded their home. The dwarfs find Snow White upstairs, asleep across three of their beds. Snow White awakes and tells them of her fate. They negotiate a little and finally settle on a shared accommodation agreement where she can remain if she cooks, cleans and sings for their entertainment.

The Queen discovers that Snow White is still alive when her magic mirror again answers that Snow White is the fairest in the land. Using magic to disguise herself as an old crone, the Queen creates a poisoned apple that will put whoever eats it into a deep death-like sleep – which can only be disturbed by 'love's first kiss'.

The Queen goes to the cottage while the dwarfs are away, but the woodland animals understand her intention (as magical woodland animals have a talent for doing) and flee to warn the dwarfs of the danger.

The Queen tricks Snow White into biting into the poisoned apple and Snow White falls asleep. The dwarfs return with the animals as the Queen leaves the cottage and the men give chase, trapping the Queen on a cliff. She tries to roll a boulder over them but before she can do so, lightning strikes the cliff, causing her to fall to her death.

The dwarfs return to their cottage to find Snow White dead, or so it seems. Unwilling to bury her, they build a glass and gold box and place her inside. They move the box to their forest clearing. Together with the magical woodland creatures, they keep watch over her.

After some time, a prince, who had previously met and fallen in love with Snow White, learns of her eternal sleep and visits her coffin. Saddened by her apparent death, he kisses her, which breaks the spell

and awakens her. The dwarfs and animals all rejoice as the Prince takes Snow White to his castle.

And they live happily ever after.

The Grimmer Tale

In the original Snow White fable, written by Jacob and Wilhelm Grimm, the Queen did not want Snow White's heart – she wanted her stepdaughter's lungs and liver. The huntsman makes the same decision, collecting the organs from a boar instead of taking Snow White's life. He brings the boar's lungs and liver to the Queen, who has them prepared by the cook and then devours them.

In the Grimm version, the Queen three times tries to kill Snow White. When she first finds out about Snow White not falling victim to the huntsman and surviving the dangers of the forest, the Queen dresses as a peddler and walks to the cottage of the dwarfs. She offers Snow White colorful, silky laced bodices and convinces the girl to take the most beautiful bodice as a present. Then the Queen laces it so tightly that Snow White faints. The Queen assumes the girl is dead and leaves triumphantly. But the dwarfs return just in time, realize the danger of the laces, and Snow White revives once they are undone.

After checking with her magic mirror, the Queen is disgusted that the job is still not finished and returns to the forest the next day in a different disguise with a poisoned comb. The Queen tricks Snow White into letting her place the comb in her hair and Snow White falls down unconscious.

The Queen rushes away, not knowing if the dwarfs will arrive in time to pull out the comb before the poison has a full effect.

The next morning, she checks with the magic mirror and hears the bad news that Snow White is still alive. She goes into her secret room and pulls out her book of spells and creates a poisoned apple. Dressing as a farmer, she convinces Snow White to eat the apple.

In the Grimm version, after the dwarfs place Snow White in the glass coffin, a prince traveling through the land sees her and falls in love. The dwarfs succumb to his request to let him have the coffin, and as his servants carry the coffin away, they stumble on tree roots. The jostling causes the piece of poisoned apple to dislodge from Snow White's throat and she wakens.

The Prince declares his love for her and a wedding is planned. The couple invites every queen and king to come to the wedding party, including Snow White's step-mother. The Queen still believes that Snow White is dead, but still asks her magical mirror who is the fairest in the land. The mirror says; "You, my queen, are fair so true. But the young Queen is a thousand times fairer than you".

The Queen is furious that after getting rid of Snow White, there is a new rival. Not knowing that this new queen was indeed her stepdaughter, she arrives at the wedding. Her heart fills with the deepest of dread when she realizes the truth.

As a punishment for the three attempts on the princess's life, a pair of glowing-hot iron shoes are brought forth with tongs and placed before the Queen. She is forced to step into the burning shoes and to dance until she drops dead.

They don't call them Grimm for nothing.

Snow White - Rewritten

We have seen Snow White and the evil queen many times since Disney's 1937 version - in movies, television series and on the stage. In each instance, Snow White is the innocent, younger woman and the Queen, the older, jealous sort, focused on protecting something that she possesses.

The TV series, *Once Upon A Time*, features fairy tale characters that bounce back and forth between a land of fairy tales and a place in the real, modern world. Snow White, Prince Charming, and the Evil Queen are featured as the main characters of the weekly drama. The evil Queen character is played as the evil queen in the fairy tale land

and as a manipulating mayor in the current world. Snow White plays a caring teacher in the modern world. In both worlds, the older woman is played as envious, unjust, controlling and evil. The younger woman is played as caring, sacrificing and naturally beautiful.

The 2012 film, *Mirror Mirror,* stars Julia Roberts as the evil Queen Clementianna and Lily Collins as Snow White. Through magic, the Queen punishes Snow White, maintains her own beauty, and casts a love spell on the much younger Prince Andrew Alcott. The older woman is played as jealous, deceitful and grasping. The younger woman is played as inventive, talented, and naturally beautiful.

The Moral of the Story

After the success of their film, *Snow White and the Seven Dwarfs,* the two brothers, Walt and Roy bought their parents a new home near the studio in Burbank, California. Shortly after moving in, Walt's mother, Flora, told him that there was a problem with the gas furnace. It was repaired, but not well, and shortly after the furnace repair, Flora died of asphyxiation caused by the fumes.

In many of the Disney princess movies, the tone is immediately set with making the viewer aware that the main character is beautiful, but motherless. Some researchers believe that Disney, who lost his mother so shortly after the success of Snow White and The Seven Dwarfs, identified with the motherless main character and many of his animated movies portrayed motherless female characters from that point on.

Not only are many of Disney's young female characters adrift without a mother's love, they are plagued by cruel older women who would like to see them suffer, even die. As the older female characters' beauty is ravaged by time and age, they become even more evil and grasping.

There are several messages that this story, in its many versions, teach us:

Women who are the most beautiful will be prized, even in death.

The Disney princesses were so beautiful, even if they were thought to be dead, men still wanted to kiss them. In the story of Sleeping Beauty, the prince kissed a beautiful woman who he thought might be dead. In Snow White, the prince did as well. In Snow White, the prince thought a woman's beauty was so significant, he wanted to take her body home to admire. When brought into today's context, these behaviours would guarantee most men a trip to the psyche ward.

Throughout the Disney movies, beauty as the avenue to happiness is overemphasized. The character Belle in the Disney animated film, *Beauty and the Beast*, is acknowledged as being a beauty, but she is as noted for being peculiar as she reads and dreams of grand adventures. Her curiosity for learning is seen as a negative characteristic that can only be mitigated by her great beauty. Snow White's primary positive characteristic is her black hair, red lips and white skin. The first gift given by the fairies in Sleeping Beauty is beauty. Good endings come to beautiful women – and they live happily ever after.

Disney princesses consistently possess pouty lips, shapely hips, non-existent waists, flowing hair, large eyes, ample busts, dainty feet and long legs. Sharon Stoner, who was the live model used by Disney for Ariel in *The Little Mermaid* and Belle in *Beauty and the Beast* is 5'2" and less than 90 pounds. Just as the Barbie doll would possess an unrealistic body if she was a real person, adult women weighing less than 90 pounds is an unrealistic and very unhealthy goal.

Expect that if you are a young and beautiful woman, other women will dislike and sabotage your success.

In a 1980s television commercial for Procter & Gamble's Pantene Pro-V 2-in-1 shampoo and conditioning formula, actress Kelly

Block shook her bountiful locks and gazed into the camera and said "Don't hate me because I am beautiful", creating a catchphrase that is anchored in the consciousness of every woman over 45.

In the business world, women don't expect other women to be their supporters. Older women judge younger women harshly based on what they wear and how they wear it. Younger women think that older women are overly harsh and condemning.

Women compete with each other on beauty and see the chase as an individual, not a team, sport. The fact that the Miss America beauty contest still occurs shows the continuing emphasis on female beauty in spite of our world becoming more equitable in other ways.

When younger women believe that other women will not be supportive, they don't ask for guidance or mentoring, and older women don't think to offer it.

You would think with all these negative consequences, women would all be walking around with paper bags over their heads. But the price of beauty - envy, hate and danger is not as important as the payout: the woman that is the most beautiful will be protected and desired by men.

The 'there-is-only-one-beauty-queen' idealism that began with the Snow White myth continues today in our relationships with other women. We are socialized to be individual competitors, with gossip, spite and destruction as our tools in winning the beauty prize. We don't really value winning the Miss Congeniality prize, we want the crown.

The desire for beauty and to be the most beautiful, combined with our socialization as young women to be envious and hateful of women who are beautiful (and distasteful and condescending to those women who are not), builds immense fences between women - making it very difficult to be caring individuals with each other.

7

BEAUTY AND THE BEAST
IT IS YOUR DUTY TO CHANGE HIM

Disney Version

Disney's *Beauty and the Beast* was released in 1991. This American animated musical film was based on the traditional fairy tale written by French novelist Jeanne-Marie Leprince de Beaumont and published in 1756.

An enchantress, disguised as a beggar, tests the character of a prince by offering him a rose in exchange for shelter from the cold, but the prince refuses. She retaliates by transforming him into a beast, and his servants into household items. She gives him a magic mirror to allow him to view faraway places and events, along with the enchanted rose that she had originally offered. To break the curse of the beast, the prince must learn to love another and earn her love in return before the last petal of the enchantress's rose falls. If the rose petals all fall before he does so, he will be a beast forever.

In a town a day's ride day away lives Belle, a young bookworm ridiculed by everyone for her desire for learning with the exceptions of her inventor father Maurice and a vain and arrogant suitor Gaston. (Even though she has repeatedly rejected his marriage offers, Gaston is determined to marry Belle.)

One day, Maurice gets lost in the forest while traveling to a fair to present his wood-chopping machine. After being chased by a pack of wolves, he comes across the Beast's castle. Rushing inside, he is quickly discovered by the Beast and detained. Maurice's horse, frightened by the Beast within and the wolves without, flees and returns home. He leads Belle to the Beast's castle where she offers to take her father's place. The Beast accepts Belle's offer and Maurice returns to town to unsuccessfully convince the townspeople to take up arms and save Belle from the Beast.

While wandering in the house, Belle enters the West Wing, an area which the Beast has told her is off limits. When he discovers her there, she flees the house to the forest where she is confronted by a pack of wolves. The Beast fends off the wolves but is injured. Belle thanks him for saving her life. He begins to develop feelings for her while she nurses his wounds. He delights her, in turn, by sharing his extensive library.

Meanwhile, Gaston thinks that Belle's father is either lying or hallucinating about the existence of the Beast and Belle's location and plots to send Belle's father to the town's insane asylum if she refuses Gaston's next marriage proposal. Maurice, frustrated and desperate, heads off to save Belle himself.

Belle tells the Beast she misses her father. The Beast allows her to use his magic mirror to see her father. She sees Maurice dying in the woods trying to rescue her. The Beast lets her go so she can save her father, giving her the mirror to remember him by. She finds Maurice and takes him home.

Gaston still doubts Maurice's sanity and the reason for Beauty's continued absence and makes plans to drag Maurice to the insane asylum. Belle proves Maurice's sanity by showing the existence of the Beast with the magic mirror. Realizing Belle loves the Beast, Gaston traps Belle and her father in their basement and leads a posse of villagers to the castle to kill the Beast.

Having stowed away into Belle's baggage, Chip, a magic chipped teacup, frees Belle and her father. Gaston confronts the Beast while the servants (candlesticks, brooms, and other equally fierce items) fend off the villagers. On the rooftop, the Beast battles and defeats Gaston, sparing his life and ordering him to leave. When the Beast's attention turns to Belle, Gaston mortally wounds the Beast, before losing his balance and falling to his death. Belle professes her love for the Beast, who dies before the last rose petal falls. With the spell broken, the Beast is returned to his human form, as are all of his servants. Belle is last seen dancing with him in the ballroom as everyone else watches in delight.

No doubt they live happy ever after.

The French Tale

The original tale of *Beauty and the Beast* was written by the French author and teacher Jeanne-Marie Leprince de Beaumont. After a disastrous first marriage and her husband's death, she moved to England to be a governess in London. It was there she wrote *Beauty and the Beast and Other Classic French Fairy Tales*. After a successful publishing career in England, she remarried, had a large family and returned to France to live the rest of her life in Savoy.

Previous stories of what we have come to think of as fairy tales today were targeted to adults. In their earliest forms (prior to Disney intervention), they were often full of death, torture, kidnapping and rape. Leprince de Beaumont was one of the first authors to write fairy tales specifically for children.

Leprince de Beaumont's tale goes like this: Beauty lived with her merchant father and her two beautiful sisters. All three young women are beautiful, but where Beauty is pure of heart, her sisters are vain, selfish, wicked and treat Beauty poorly.

Our story begins with Beauty's father discovering that all of his ships, but one, have sunk. He is going to the port himself to ensure the safe sale of goods from his final ship. Before leaving, he asks his three daughters what they would like purchased for them from the proceeds of the sale. The two eldest ask for fine dresses and jewels. Beauty only wants a red rose, if he can find one, as they are not common in the area where they live.

His trip was successful in that his ship has returned, but alas the ship's cargo has been seized to pay his debts. He set out on his journey home without gifts for any of his three daughters. He gets lost in a forest. (Apparently the cliché that men do not ask for directions dates back over 250 years).

Eventually, he comes to a lovely castle where every window has a light blazing. He thinks it must be the home of a nobleman and perchance he might receive supper and a night's lodging. He knocks, the doors open, but no one is standing there. He enters and calls out, but no reply comes. He goes into the dining room and sits down at a setting for one. He says to himself, "I think this castle is enchanted. I'll see if there is anyone upstairs." He found no one but discovers a bedroom with a turned down quilt and a steaming hot bath. He enjoys the bath and immediately falls asleep.

The next morning he wakes to find his clothing laundered and pressed, and a breakfast laid out. He toasts his invisible host and servants, eats, and prepares to be on his way. He gathers his bag, collects his horse and takes off down the drive.

Along the drive are hundreds of rose bushes. Remembering Beauty's request, he dismounts and selects the most red and luscious bloom. When he picks it, he hears a great roar and a Beast jumps out of the shadows. "I gave you everything and you steal my roses!" roars the Beast.

The Beast insists that all thieves must die, but the merchant begs to be set free, explaining about his youngest daughter's request. The beast agrees to let him give the rose to Beauty, but only if the merchant will return.

The merchant is upset, but accepts the condition. The Beast sends him on his way.

The merchant returns home (along the right road this time) and tries to hide the events from his daughters. Beauty pries the secret from him and he tells the tale to his daughters. The two eldest daughters say nothing, but Beauty offers to go to the Beast in her father's stead.

The Beast receives her graciously and informs her that she is now mistress of the castle and he, her servant. He gives her lavish clothing and carries on lengthy conversations with her each evening over dinner. Every night, the Beast asks Beauty to marry him, only to be refused each time.

Alone in her luxurious bed, each night Beauty dreams of a handsome prince who pleads with her to answer why she keeps refusing the Beast. She becomes convinced that the Beast is holding the prince captive somewhere in the castle. She searches but never finds the prince from her dreams.

Beauty becomes homesick and begs the Beast to allow her to go see her family. He allows it on the condition that she returns exactly a week later. Beauty agrees to this and sets off for home with an enchanted mirror and ring. The mirror allows her to see events at the castle and the ring allows her to return to the castle in an instant when turned three times around her finger.

Her older sisters are surprised to find her well fed and dressed in finery. They are envious when they hear of her happy life at the castle, and, hearing that she must return to the Beast on a certain day, beg her to stay another day and put onion in their eyes to make it appear as though they are weeping. They hope that the Beast will be angry with Beauty for breaking her promise and eat her alive. Beauty's heart is moved by her sisters' false show of love, and she agrees to stay.

Several days pass and when Beauty finally looks into her magic mirror, she is shocked to see in the reflection that the Beast is dying. She immediately uses the ring to return to his side. She weeps, crying that she loved him. When her tears strike his face, he is magically transformed into his former handsome self, her love having saved him.

He and Beauty are married and they live happily ever after together.

Moral of the Story - Duty, Change and 50 Shades of Grey

The moral that comes immediately to mind is that if men would only ask directions, they would not be required to sacrifice their daughters to beasts. But there are three other lessons that women learn from this tale: to be dutiful, to help your man change, and to tolerate violent behaviour.

Duty

One of the messages presented in this story is duty, teaching that it is desirous to sacrifice oneself for the safety and lives of parents and family. Beauty knew for her father's sake, she "had to be brave, that crying would not help me, nor despair."

Change

Another effect of this fairy tale on women is that it leads us to believe that if we love a man enough, he can change - he can be anything. It teaches young women that it is their duty to bring out the prince in their fellow - to look for a man's potential - not just what you see today.   That without a woman's help, a man is incomplete and needs a woman's love and attention to be released from his beastliness.

The change may be superficial. I remember that when I married my husband, Malcolm, I had a goal to get him to quit wearing tweeds and plaid sports jackets in favour of double breasted, solid coloured suits. He's a tall broad-shouldered fellow and his wardrobe at the time made him look, well, boxlike. "He's a great guy - and by the time I'm done with him he will be a well-dressed, great guy!"

The change may be economical. Women fall in love with the potential of a man - what he can be. "Sure he's working at Wal-Mart at the moment, but he'll be a CEO one day."

Women sometimes believe that underneath it all, their husbands or boyfriends really are princes - handsome, well-dressed, successful and romantic. They think if they try hard enough, they can discover the prince in their men and the sloppy clothes, yesterday's beard, and today's lack of desire to mow the lawn will peel away. They are willing to do what needs to be done to manifest the transformation, possessing an attitude that men are like houses that are "fixer uppers" - they can be wallpapered and painted and if necessary, gutted.

Endure

Beauty said, "I must find the courage to endure."

This fairy tale can also teach women that if we find ourselves in a relationship with a partner who is disrespectful or violent, we don't leave, we stay. In Disney's tale, Belle is frightened enough by the Beast that she runs away and risks being attacked by wolves rather than his violent nature – yet she remains.

We hope we can change him, and nobly remain, telling ourselves that change is just around the corner, that is - "if we don't despair, if we have enough courage."

No modern tale has done as good a job of encouraging us to remain in a violent relationship than the novel, *Fifty Shades of Grey*.

Fifty Shades of Grey is a 2011 erotic romance novel by British author E. L. James which explores a relationship between a college

graduate, Anastasia Steele, and a young business magnate, Christian Grey. The book topped best-seller lists around the world, including those of the UK and USA. It has been translated into 52 languages and set a record in the UK as the fastest-selling paperback of all time.

The movie, *Fifty Shades of Grey,* released in 2015, was an immediate success, breaking numerous box office records and earning

over $569 million worldwide. It is currently the seventh-highest-grossing film of 2015.

Just as did Disney's Cinderella movie, this movie has shaped our society.

Ana Steele is a 21-year-old college senior. Her best friend, Kate, who writes for the college newspaper, is unable to interview 27-year-old wealthy entrepreneur (Christian Grey) and asks Ana to take her place. Ana finds Christian attractive but also intimidating. She does not expect to meet Christian again, but he shortly appears at the hardware store where she works. Ana informs Christian that Kate would likesome photographs to go along with her article about him and Christian gives Ana his phone number. The next day the photographer, Kate, and Ana arrive for the photo shoot at the hotel where Christian is staying. Following the photo shoot, Christian asks Ana out for coffee.

Ana learns that Christian is single, but he says he is no romantic. She is intrigued but believes she is not attractive enough for Christian. Later that night, Ana goes out drinking with her friends and ends up calling Christian, who informs her that he will be coming to

pick her up because of her inebriated state. Later, Ana wakes to find herself in Christian's hotel room, where he scolds her for not taking proper care of herself. He reveals that he would like to have sex with her, but in alignment with his stated lack of romantic thought, he wants Ana to fill out paperwork first.

Christian insists that she sign a non-disclosure agreement forbidding her to discuss anything that they do together, which Ana agrees to sign. He also informs her that the second contract will be one of dominance and submission and that there will be no romantic relationship, only a sexual one. The contract even forbids Ana from touching Christian or making eye contact with him. At this point, Christian realizes that Ana is a virgin and agrees to have sex without making her sign the contract – which they do.

Over the next few days, Ana receives several gifts from Christian. Ana meets up with Christian to discuss the contract, only to grow overwhelmed by the potential BDSM (bondage, dominance, submission, masochism) arrangement and the potential of having a sexual relationship with Christian that is not romantic in nature. Ana runs away from Christian and does not see him again until her college graduation, where he is a guest speaker. The two meet up to further discuss the contract and Ana is spanked for the first time by Christian. The experience leaves her more attracted to him but confused. Her confusion is exacerbated by Christian's lavish gifts, and the fact that he brings her to meet his family. The tension between Ana and Christian eventually comes to a head after Ana asks Christian to punish her in order to show her how extreme a BDSM relationship with him could be. Christian fulfils Ana's request, beating her with a belt, only for Ana to realize that the two of them are incompatible. Devastated, Ana leaves.

This version of the Beauty and the Beast fairy tale teaches women that:

Violence is sexy and so is sexual brokenness. Ana and Christian's relationship is not one just of kinky sex, but one of abuse. In 2013, in a study conducted by Bonomi and Altenburger, *Fifty Shades of Grey* was read by multiple professionals and assessed for characteristics of intimate partner violence. They found that nearly every interaction between Ana and Christian was emotionally abusive in nature, including stalking, intimidation, and isolation. The study group also observed pervasive sexual violence, including Christian's use of alcohol to circumvent Ana's ability to consent, and that Ana exhibits classic signs of an abused woman, including constant perceived threat, stressful managing, and altered identity.

Women should put up with stalkers. When Grey shows up at her workplace and later in the book/film at her parents' house in Georgia where she is visiting, she is surprised. If Christian Grey had been overweight, bald, poor, and worked for the Post office, do you think that Ana would have allowed the stalking and abuse? Or would she have kicked him to the curb?

8

DISNEY'S CRIPPLING INFLUENCE CONTINUES

In childhood, we develop beliefs about gender roles and one of the primary contributors to that understanding is the media of television and film. According to the American Academy of Pediatrics, not only do the characters' words and actions influence gender roles, the songs the characters sing are a powerful conscious and subconscious influence. Therefore, Disney, with its plethora of animated, child-targeted feature films has a wide influence on how women develop their beliefs about gender roles and understanding of how women should speak, believe and act.

Researchers Kristine Hoover, Molly Pepper and Lazarina Topuzova investigated whether the influence of Disney's songs have increased or decreased positive gender roles for women. It is very disappointing what their research concluded, both for women in general, and specifically for women as leaders.

Gender roles express society's expectations for the specific behaviours that are considered appropriate for each gender. Researchers Eagly and Johannesen-Schmidt isolated characteristics as

of 'agentic' (from the term agent meaning a person who exerts power or an effect) to men and 'communal' to women. Agentic (male) leadership characteristics are often seen as assertive, controlling, and confident. Communal (female) leadership characteristics are often focused on others (concerns for the people she leads or influences).

However, as researchers Eagly and Johannesen-Schmidt stated many times in their research, the characteristics that we often describe as leadership qualities are more closely aligned with agentic behaviours than communal behaviours – meaning that gender roles for women are misaligned with leadership behaviours according to society's rules for gender.

It is not as simple as women leaders merely behaving like male leaders. That has been tried, and we have discovered that when a female leader behaves like a male leader, she is often seen in a negative light. Bossy, not a boss. Pushy, not persuasive. Selfish if she is working late, not dedicated to the organization.

It is true that we are discussing new leadership theories such as servant leadership which are in alignment with a communal leadership style. However, because men have traditionally held the leadership positions in politics, government and the workplace, they have defined the type of behaviours that people associate with good leadership – autonomy, directness, and competitiveness. Women's approach to leadership (characteristics described as caring, nurturing, collaborative, considerate and supportive) is seen as a different and less valid leadership style. The 'Catch 22' for women is that they often cannot rise to the ceiling of their organizational chart using a communal style of leadership, but if they use an agentic style – they are less liked and respected.

Of course, gender roles do not begin once a woman is in the workplace. Our gender roles began the day our mothers place us in blue pajamas or pink nighties.

In the previous four chapters, we discussed the four iconic Disney princess animated films. You may believe that Disney princess movies have become more gender neutral and girl positive over the past decades, but when we look closely at new research we see that we may be actually going backwards in this regard. Many studies have been written examining the impact of Disney movies relating to gender, race, ethnicity, age, and sexuality. But until the research of Hoover, Pepper and Topuzova, no research had been published on the effect and impact of the song lyrics that flow through each animated Disney film. Their research goes further and shows us that the newer animated films actually create female gender roles that are even LESS likely to align with accepted leadership style.

As mentioned earlier, the American Academy of Pediatrics state that songs, like other forms of contemporary media culture, provide an important role as originators for socialization for children and gender role development. As films are a means of imparting gendered expectations, and because socialization begins at such a young age, the characters on the screen and their behaviours are absorbed with greater intensity than if an adult was watching these movies for the first time.

Hoover, Pepper and Topuzova found that while Disney theme songs do not capture all of the multiple dimensions of socialization, exploring the gendered expectations within these songs further clarifies who society tells children they should be and what they can accomplish.

The researchers studied the lyrics from Disney's central songs to compare gendered differences between early and recent Disney fully-animated movies. The movies the songs were selected from were released by Walt Disney Productions (prior to 1986) or Walt Disney Animation Studios (1986 and later). A central song was one that described or was the theme song for the movie - a song that most accurately described the crux of the entire plot. (See appendix A for the full list of the movies and songs included in the study.)

The researchers asked: Over the years, has the level of active tone changed in how Disney movies socialize gender and leadership roles? (Active tone was measured by the percentage of very active words minus the percentage of very passive words.)

The active tone in songs sung by female lead characters before 1986 was -9.20, and after 1986 it was -20.45. The drop in active tone of central songs from films with a female lead appears to be caused by a higher percentage of very passive words in the central songs, not a lower percentage of very active words in the central songs. The percentage of very passive words in central songs from movies with a female lead was 13.16 before 1986 and 24.56 in or after 1986.

In other words, the song lyrics female characters sing have not significantly increased in active words (which would have been the case if Disney movies truly were becoming more female empowering).

The results of this study are particularly bad news is the increase of very passive words in songs sung by female lead characters, leading to the substantial decline in female leads' active tone since 1986. Thanks to the influence of Disney, this shift could develop a gendered expectation of passivity, which could negatively impact a woman's ability to exercise the active, directive behavior perceived to be key in leadership positions.

Even when women act through a communal frame, taking action as a leader is essential. Being assertive and confident are essential in leading organizations, especially in crisis or change.

9

MEDIA MAKES US WANT TO BE THE PERFECT PRINCESS

As women become more powerful in politics, corporations and government, one would think that there would be a corresponding increase of powerful and respectful portrayals of women in media. However, the opposite is true. With changes in US legislation starting with the 1976 Supreme Court granting 1st Amendment rights to media, the relaxation of content rules has allowed for an increase in the sexualisation of women in television shows and television advertising with a direct effect on society's perception of women.

Marketers dictate our cultural norms and values. Most media gets its revenue from advertising so non-advertising content often supports the advertising agenda. Therefore it is marketers who are dictating our cultural norms and values. Their agenda focuses on creating anxiety in their viewers (which the advertised products can alleviate) and increasing their number of viewers.

The media is delivering content that is shaping our society and our children's brains and emotions. Girls get the message early on that what is important is how they look. Boys get the message early on that they should measure a girl's value by her looks.

Even as we age, media continues to focus first on the outside of a woman, and secondly on her intellectual contribution or accomplishments. During the 2008 American political election, what women wore, how they styled their hair, and even what procedures they may have had done to their bodies was open for discussion. What was with Hillary Clinton and her pant suits? Did Sarah Palin have breast implants? Even outside of an election cycle, media treats the most powerful women in American government very harshly (Hillary looking haggard, Condoleezza Rice dressing like a dominatrix).

Even if you do not live in the USA, the proliferation and diversity of American media, through not only television but also through the internet, makes avoiding this phenomenon impossible - so we need to all understand its impact on women and leadership.

Self-Objectification

As mentioned above, media makes their money through advertising and advertising is all about creating anxiety in viewers. For women, the anxiety created is often focused on a lack of beauty, or not being beautiful enough or beautiful in the right way. This futile pursuit of the perfect body creates revenue for the providers of advertising who show female bodies that are unreal, photo-shopped and computer generated as the ideal female form.

Modern industrialized society chronically and pervasively objectifies the female body, and many women have come to view themselves through the lens of an external observer, habitually monitoring their own appearance whether in public or private settings. The negative effects associated with this 'self-objectification' are body shame, appearance anxiety, depression, and disordered eating.

How does this affect women's ability to lead? Caroline Heldman, Associate Professor of Political Science at Occidental College in California states that not only is self-objectification bad for women in general, but that the American Psychological Association found that women who have high self-objectification have low political efficacy (the idea that your voice matters in the political sphere, that you can be part of a change in politics, and that you can run for politics, and run successfully). One would think that this same dynamic would be at play with women's beliefs in their ability to lead organizations outside of politics.

Over-sexualization

60% of television viewers in the United States are women and of the remaining 40% male viewers, the 18-34 year old age group is the most difficult group to get to watch non-sports television content. The top cable non-sports series among men ages 18 to 34 is WWE Raw on the USA network and some critics would consider this fake wrestling show a type of sport. The number one cable network with the largest primetime viewership among men ages 18 to 34 is ESPN with an average of 343,000 men watching at any given time.

The most effective way to attract this age group to non-sport content is with over-sexualized advertising content and core content. Not only do the commercials show scantily clad women, often moving in a sexual way, it also leads to sexualization within the core content of a show. Consider the female news broadcasters on FOX News with more cleavage exposed than one would expect from a female server in a cocktail bar.

Who is in charge?

Media is overwhelmingly in the hands of men. Women only own 5.8% of the television stations in the United States, and only 6% of the radio stations. When we look at who is behind the scenes making the decisions, we see that all the major media organizations are led by men and their boards of directors are weighted heavily with men:

- The Walt Disney Company (Robert Iger, CEO)
  Board composition: 4 Women/9 Men
- GE/NBC (Jeffrey T. Immelt, CEO)
  Board composition: 4 Women/13 Men
- Viacom/MTV (Phillip Dauman, CEO)
  Board composition: 2 Women/9 Men
- Time Warner (Jeffrey L. Bewkes, CEO)
  Board composition: 2 Women/11 Men
- CBS (Les Mooves)
  Board composition: 2 Women/12 Men

This is big, big business and change that is not about increasing shareholder value will be slow in coming. Advertisers spent $235.6 billion in television advertising in 2009 alone – which is more than the GDP of 80% of the countries in the world.

10

CHOOSE DIFFERENT DECISIONS

In the previous chapters, we discussed our history and the forces of media and myth that have brought us to this place.

Wouldn't it be easy if we could find some of that magic so prevalent in the fairy tales to change the situation, for us as individual women, and for women in general?

Alas, as they say in many a fairy tale, that is not to be. Therefore we must, after recognizing how we got where we are today, begin to take different actions on a daily basis to support not only other women in becoming powerful leaders, but in assisting ourselves in that goal as well.

The following chapter address essential keys to creating powerful women leaders. These are not all the keys, but they will put you on a good track to success if you take actions recommended.

11

CHOOSE MEDIA THAT SUPPORTS FEMALE REPRESENTATION

What do Smurfette, Miss Piggy and Penny of Big Bang Theory fame have in common? The Smurfette Principle.

The Smurfette Principle is the tendency for works of fiction to have exactly one female amongst an ensemble of male characters, in spite of the fact that roughly half of the human race is female. Smurfette was the only female Smurf, Miss Piggy was the only female Muppet and at the beginning of the show, Penny was the singular Smurfette across the hall from the ensemble of smart male scientists.

This phenomenon is closely related to the Bechdel Test (or the Mo Movie measure). The Bechdel test is a litmus test to measure the presence of women in movies. How well are they represented in relation to their overall population. The test asks three simple questions:

- Does this movie have at least two women in it who have names?
- Do they talk to each other?
- Do they talk about a subject other than a man?

Surprisingly, many movies that you think are supportive to women, fail this test of minimal representation of women. Consider the following list of failed movies, according to Bechdel:

Slumdog Millionaire
Shrek
Bourne Identity
Ghostbusters
Austin Powers 1, 2 and 3
Men in Black
The Fifth Element
The Princess Bride
The Wedding Singer
Shawshank Redemption
Lord of the Rings 1, 2 and 3
The Truman Show
Mission Impossible
Braveheart
Toy Story
When Harry Met Sally
Back to the Future 1, 2 and 3
Tomb Raider

Pulp Fiction
Home Alone
Up

Even when we look at the nominations for best film for the 2011 Oscars, only two of the films pass the Bechtel test.

War Horse - fail
The Artist - fail
Descendants - pass
Extremely Loud and Incredibly Close - fail
The Help - pass
Midnight in Paris - fail
Moneyball - fail
Tree of Life - fail
Hugo - fail

Only *The Help* and *The Descendants* pass the Bechtel Test.

As discussed earlier in this book, the film and media industry is highly dominated by men. This leads to a systemic problem where films are made primarily to cater to men and are about men.

When you attend a film, go in with the three questions of the Bechdel in mind. Encourage others to attend films that show that women are indeed 50% of the population. Choose movies that make you feel included, intelligent, strong and courageous.

12

CHOOSE AN EMPLOYER
WITH GRIT

When you are interviewing for a position, do you ask about their commitment to gender equality or diversity? Do you think even bringing up the issue would mean to the interviewer that you are looking for some kind of special treatment? Might it suggest you are an overenthusiastic advocate?

But how do you find out about a company's true commitment to equality? How do you find out if they have the kind of grit that would make you want to commit to working for them? A business-focused way of addressing this issue is to ask them if they have heard of the Women's Empowerment Principles and whether they have signed on.

The Women's Empowerment Principles, or WEPs, are a set of principles for business offering guidance on how to empower women

in the workplace, marketplace and community. Focused on business, the WEPs provide a clear and comprehensive approach to achieving gender equality. Even taking small steps within one of the principles could make a big difference.

Organizations can have their chief officer sign the CEO Statement of Support for the WEPs, which would show executive commitment and example. An organization could use the principles to assess initiatives and company policies. They may even develop a strategy to integrate a gender lens into existing reporting mechanisms. There are guidelines that address training, reporting, community involvement and policy development.

A collaboration between the United Nations Entity for Gender Equality and the Empowerment of Women (UN Women) and the United Nations Global Compact, these guidelines emphasize the business case for corporate commitment to promote gender equality. The subtitle of the guidelines is EQUALITY MEANS BUSINESS because the WEPs are based on real-life business practices and input gathered from across the globe.

The Women's Empowerment Principles seek to point the way to best practice and act as a useful guide for businesses that work towards gender equality, but don't know where to start or even if they are using the most useful strategies.

Here are the seven WEP:

- **Principle 1: Establish high-level corporate leadership for gender equality**
- **Principle 2: Treat all women and men fairly at work – respect and support human rights and non-discrimination**

- **Principle 3: Ensure the health, safety and well-being of all women and men workers**

- **Principle 4: Promote education, training and professional development for women**

- **Principle 5: Implement enterprise development, supply chain and marketing practices that empower women**

- **Principle 6: Promote equality through community initiatives and advocacy**

- **Principle 7: Measure and publicly report on progress to achieve gender equality**

If you had to evaluate your current organization against these principles, how would it measure up?

13

CHOOSE A GENDER NEUTRAL LEADERSHIP MODEL

It doesn't matter whether you drive a Mercedes AMG GT or a Dodge Dart, all four of your tires need to be inflated to the correct psi (pounds per square inch) and equally balanced. If one of your tires is flat, or seriously deflated, you will not be driving anywhere. Or at least not safely or without creating damage to other parts of your vehicle.

Just as you possess four physical tires on your Dart or GT, you have four invisible tires to your leadership and if any one of your leadership tires are over-inflated or deflated, you will fail as a leader.

Consider your front tires. Your driver's side front tire is courage and your passenger's side front tire is insight. Your rear driver's side tire is self-discipline and your rear passenger's side tire is influence over others. All four must be equally inflated to proper psi if you are to be an effective, balanced leader.

With your front passenger's side tire - insight - you can think and recognize needs. Perhaps you see the need for programs to assist people in poverty in your community or a need that is not currently being filled by a business in your area.

The front driver's side tire is courage. With insight and courage, you have the initiative to talk to colleagues and friends about the needs you perceive in the community. You might discuss with others the possibility of beginning an organization to address those needs. If it is a business idea, courage will get you an appointment at your bank to negotiate a loan or the fearlessness to publicly announce that you are opening a new business.

Self-discipline, your driver's side rear tire, gives you the persistence to work through the red tape of organizing the charity that addresses hunger and poverty. With self-discipline and courage, you could methodically keep cold calling people to promote your business even after fifty such calls yielded no success.

With the final tire, influence over others, you can successfully invite others to join you in your goal – whether it is building a charity, launching a new company or running for political office.

What happens if one or more of your leadership tires are deflated?

- A person who only has insight is someone who talks about starting a business, building an organization – but never takes action on the plan.
- Courage without insight gets you to the wrong place quickly.
- Courage and insight without self-discipline may give you an initial burst of enthusiasm, but it will soon dwindle as the going gets tough.

- Self-discipline, courage and insight without influencing others makes you a leader without followers. That can be very lonely.

The recommended air pressure for tires on a car depends on the size of the vehicle. The pressure normally ranges between 28 and 36 psi (pounds per square inch). You too must be aware of what your limits are. Trying to take massive action in all four areas at one time might ensure a blowout.

The exact tire air pressure recommended by the auto manufacturer is found in at least one of three places. The first and most common is a sticker inside the driver's side door jam. The sticker lists what type of tires fit the vehicle, as well as the recommended pressure for the tires. If the sticker is not present, check the glove compartment. The same sticker should be there with the correct specifications. If all else fails, check the car's service manual, which lists all the basic maintenance information for the car. Wouldn't it be wonderful if such clear and concise directions came for our leadership tires. What we should do, at what speed and effort and with a Plan B and a Plan C.

Lowering the air pressure in a tire creates a larger area of contact between the tire and the ground and makes driving on softer ground much easier. It also does less damage to the surface of the tire. When we are overwhelmed, we can always take a little bit of air out of each of our four tires and give ourselves some time to regroup, rethink and pause.

Gandhi was a leader who had good and balanced tire pressure.

He was arrested in 1922 and charged with sedition for his articles in the publication, *Young India*. On March 23, at the end of his trial he was allowed to address the court before being sentenced to six years in jail.

"Before I read this statement, I would like to state that I entirely endorse the learned advocate general's remarks in connection with my humble self. I think that he was entirely fair to me in all the statements that he has made, because it is very true, and I have no desire whatsoever to conceal from this court the fact that to preach disaffection towards the existing system of government has become almost a passion with me; and the learned advocate general is also entirely in the right when he says that my preaching of disaffection did not commence with my connection with *Young India* but that it commenced much earlier and in the statement that I am about to read it will be my painful duty to admit before this court that it commenced much earlier than the period stated by the advocate general. It is the most painful duty with me, but I have to discharge that duty knowing the responsibility that rests upon my shoulders."

We can look at the example of Gandhi as not only a transformational leader, but a leader who demonstrated the four essentials of personal leadership. His courage to face judgment time and time again by the British courts, insisting that if they were going to incarcerate him, they should know the whole story of his civil disobedience against the crown.

His insight regarding the future of his country and what was required to gain his objective of equal rights for Indians within India was demonstrated in his other comments before the court. While living in South Africa, he had supported the British empire by serving in the Boer War, even though he was discriminated against by the British because he was an Indian.

Mahatma Gandhi's self-discipline by remaining on his path, working towards his political goals through fasts and boycotts and placing his goals before his own creature comfort, is something few of us would be willing to do.

Finally, the influence that Gandhi had over the people of India was remarkable – to remain non-violent while their world was one of violence and injustice. In Gandhi's eulogy, the Prime Minister of India commented on his influence over others:

"Great men and eminent men have monuments in bronze and marble set up for them, but this man of divine fire managed in his lifetime to become enshrined in millions and millions of hearts so that all of us became somewhat of the stuff that he was made of, though to an infinitely lesser degree. He spread out in this way all over India, not in palaces only, or in select places or assemblies, but in every hamlet and hut of the lowly and those who suffer. He lives in the hearts of millions and he will live for immemorial ages."

Keeping the correct air pressure in your tires helps your tires last longer, helps your car handle better and safer, and helps you save money on fuel. Most people forget about their tires until something goes wrong. The truth is, tires lose pressure daily. In cool weather, a tire will typically lose one or two pounds of air per month. In warm weather, tires lose even more air. That's why it's recommended that you check air pressure every other time you stop to fill up your gas tank. Keep in mind that many vehicles have different tire pressures on the front and rear axle. And don't forget to check the pressure in your spare tire.

Just like your tires on your car, you need to ensure your tires of leadership are balanced and at the correct psi – but if you are facing a tough road ahead – do yourself a favour – and lower the pressure.

14

INFLUENCE: WOMAN TALK

Women often talk in an apologetic, passive, subtly persuasive and indirect way. We do so as a learned habit, trained in this style by other women in our lives. This style of communication may hold us back from clearer and more powerful communication - yet abandoning it may also create poor relationships with both men and women who have an expectation as to how we will interact with them. The expectation of a passive, caring, and kind style is in alignment with a nice woman. Communicating like a man can be seen as acerbic, harsh, uncaring and rude.

In this chapter we will explore five of the key communication style differences that can challenge women as leaders.

#1 - Space

Wonder Woman! Xena – Warrior Princess! Two women who stand with hands on their hips, feet spread apart, face up to the sky, and to hell with the world. Also – totally imaginary characters. Both characters (besides having breasts that could poke an eye out) stand with their hands on their hips and take up space. As discussed in earlier chapters, although these two women are powerful characters in their stories, their clothing is very sexualized in the three areas most titillating – tight, slight and deep. To have portrayed such powerful women in anything but a mitigating sexual ensemble would not have been acceptable in our perfect body media world.

Powerful people take up more physical space than people who are less powerful or who feel less powerful. Think about how women sit - legs crossed or ankles crossed and pulled back. We often sit with our arms crossed (and not because we are cold, bored, or have a broken bra strap). We sit with our hands in our laps or around an object.

Men are more likely than women to sprawl their arm across the back of a chair beside them or prop their feet up on a desk edge. They are also more likely to cross their ankle over their opposite knee. These maneuvers take up space and are used - consciously or unconsciously - by men to infer authority.

It is easy to begin taking up more space, but be cautious in overdoing your reach. Think about using arm rests instead of holding your hands closely together. Use coffee tables for coffee cups and leave yourself open to being more expressive with gestures.

As well as your horizontal space, consider your use of vertical space. If someone comes into your workspace and stands in front of you or behind you, the difference in height works in their favour - especially in negotiating. Ask the person to sit down. If they insist on standing, find a reason to stand yourself (finding something in a file cabinet) so the disadvantage is mitigated.

#2 - Head Bobble

Most women nod their heads when they are listening. Men of European descent nod their heads only if they agree with the speaker, rarely to merely signal they are paying attention. (Men from Asian countries might also nod to signify their attention.)

This might seem like a small difference, but could quickly lead to miscommunication. A man may believe that a woman agrees with his opinion or idea simply because she is nodding. Alternately, a woman might also believe a man is not listening because he is not nodding.

A secondary head movement that women make is that they often tilt their head to one side when listening. This is a submissive stance and minimizes men's perceptions of your confidence and competence. Looking at photographic business head shots of men and women, notice how often the picture of the man is straight on and the woman is from a tilted head position. If a photographer asks you to tilt your head in a business photo, refuse.

#3 - Apologizing

Women use apologetic language for a variety of situations: when they bump into someone (Pardon me), when they miscommunicate (I'm sorry, I thought we were doing it this way), when they drop something (I'm sorry, I'll get that out of your way) - with the most damaging of these being apologizing for miscommunicating.

If men bump into someone or something, they are more likely to use words like "oops" or "watch out". Men rarely apologize for misunderstanding or miscommunication. They use the term "I'm sorry" more sparingly because they equate those words to a true apology, not just a smoothing of communication.

As we mentioned earlier when discussing mentoring, women value equality in relationships. Therefore if a woman apologizes to another woman, the other woman usually balances out the apology by taking some of the responsibility with comments like "Oh, it was my fault too," "Oh, that's alright", "It's understandable, it is so crowded in here", or "Who put that chair there anyway?"

It is almost as if a woman is unbalanced, standing with her arm outstretched in supplication, waiting until the other person in the communication leans forward to take her hand and stabilized her. If a woman apologizes to a man, unless he really is sorry, he is unlikely to create that balance. "I'm sorry" may be met with "Well, you should plan more carefully in the future."

This can lead to women thinking men are uncaring and men thinking women don't stand up for themselves or are weak. As a leader, think carefully as to how you use the words, "I'm sorry". If you want to develop a relationship with another woman, especially one who has less economic status in your organization, it is important to retain the balancing of apology situations. With men, even switching from using "I'm sorry" to "Pardon me" will increase your credibility and power.

#4 – Up talk

For English speakers, our ear is trained to interpret an uplift at the end of the sentence to mean a question. What you do with your last syllable affects your influence on your audience, whether it is an audience of one or a hundred. By lifting your last syllable, you infer a question as if you are searching for agreement or are looking for information or advice. If this is not your intent, you risk a loss of credibility.

By maintaining the same tone with the last syllable of your last word, you make a statement, albeit in a neutral way. By lowering the last syllable of the last word, you infer authority and command.

When we lift our last syllables of our sentences, our audience perceives a question even though we are making a statement. This can lead the listener to question the authority of the speaker. "Does she really know what she is talking about?"

When we are attempting to increase our credibility, we must be diligent about maintaining an even or lowered tone at the end of our statements. The effect of uptalk cannot be underestimated.

#5 - Indirectness of Speech

If a woman says: "Do you want to pick up milk on the way home?" or "Could you stop and pick up milk on the way home?", she means "I need you to pick up milk. Will you?"

If a women says: "Don't you find it cold in here?", "Is it chilly in here?", "I wonder if the furnace is working?", she means "Turn up the heat."

Men shake their heads, thinking they will never understand women.

This communication difference causes enough problems in our personal lives but how it affects our success in the workplace can be significant. A female leader who refuses to communicate directly with her subordinates may find herself with a team that doesn't perform because they think her directives are suggestions.

She says: It would be nice if I got this report by Thursday.
She means: I need the report by Thursday.
He hears: You can do the report anytime, but Thursday would be nice.

She says: I like the report but I have a few suggestions or changes you may want to make before you send it to head office.

She means: It's good but make these changes before you send it to head office.

He hears: Looks good - send it the way it is if you want.

Women in these situations might honestly believe that their staff are undermining them or not taking their authority seriously. What could easily be happening is their indirect communication style is not being interpreted accurately.

When women leaders succeed in blue collar environments (particularly industrial), they have managed to talk like those in their environment. Consciously or unconsciously, they have picked up a more direct style of communication. The men they work with might say that their female leader "speaks their language" and "just says what's on her mind."

Some male leaders boast that they treat everyone the same. What that really means is that they treat everyone like themselves. They communicate to everyone the way they would like to be communicated to. People naturally prefer to work with (and promote) people who are like themselves and with whom they feel comfortable. Women are at an immediate disadvantage if they communicate in an indirect way and report to a direct communicator.

It is important to ask ourselves what our goal is in communication and to then adjust our style or approach accordingly. Not only is it important to speak in a direct style with men, it is equally important to be flexible enough to bounce back to a more indirect style with women. Women are used to other women functioning in an indirect communication style with them. When a woman communicates in a direct style, it often confuses or puts off other women. They might even find a direct communication style coming from another woman caustic and abrasive.

15

INSIGHT: WRITE NEW CODE

I walk down the street.
There is a deep hole in the sidewalk.
I fall in.
I am lost...I am hopeless.
It isn't my fault.
It takes forever to find a way out.

I walk down the same street.
There is a deep hole in the sidewalk.
I pretend I don't see it.
I fall in again.
I can't believe I am in the same place.
But it isn't my fault.
It still takes a long time to get out.

I walk down the same street.

There is a deep hole in the sidewalk.

I see it is there.

I still fall in …it's a habit.

My eyes are open.

I know where I am.

It is my fault.

I get out immediately.

I walk down the same street.

There is a deep hole in the sidewalk.

I walk around it.

I walk down another street.

Leaders must not only be learning about their organization and industry, they must be learning about learning. This poem above, called *Autobiography In Five Chapters*, appeared in Kenneth Ring's book, *Heading Towards Omega: In Search of the Meaning of the Near Death Experience* (1985) and was retold in *The Tibetan Book of Living and Dying* by Sognal Rinpoche.

In the first walk, the author he sees himself as a depressed victim. "I am lost, I am hopeless, it isn't my fault," he laments. Leaders do not have the luxury of blaming others or circumstances. Pitying ourselves when a situation goes the wrong direction services no one, and delays positive movement.

In the second walk he sees himself as frustrated and helpless to control his situation. "I can't believe I am in the same place. But it isn't my fault," he complains. By not focusing on how he ended up in the hole, he can't yet learn how to avoid the danger or change the outcome.

In the third walk he sees himself as stuck in his reality, but seeing possibilities. "I still fall in …it's a habit. My eyes are open. I know where I am. It is my fault," he whispers to himself. He can see that there is now hope and takes action immediately.

In the fourth walk, he sees himself as being able to make adjustments. "I walk around it," he boasts.

But in the fifth walk, we see that he has truly learned. "I went down another street," he comments, no doubt with a smile.

Toni Newman, an innovation coach in Canada, believes that leaders need to be continuously creating innovative value, demonstrating innovative value and delivering innovative value. She challenges her clients to evaluate to what degree they are researching and creating new code that is provocative, genuine, theirs alone and absolutely true. In other words, how are you becoming a better learner and therefore a better leader? What are you learning that takes you not only around your problems, but down an entirely different street?

16

SELF DISCIPLINE: EVEN WHEN THE GOING GETS TOUGH

Florence Nightingale Graham was born in Woodbridge, Ontario in 1882, the daughter of a Scottish vegetable peddler and horse racer. She had a vision to be the richest woman in the world.

While working at a hospital (training to become a nurse – with two first names of Florence Nightingale, you can see what her parents dreams were for her), she met a biochemist who was working on a skin cream remedy for acne. This led her to experiment with beauty products in her own family kitchen laboratory. When her experiments became so particularly odoriferous that the neighbours thought the family had been reduced financially to cooking rotten eggs, Florence's father advised her to get a real job.

She moved to New York City and got a job as a bookkeeper for Squibb Pharmaceutical Company, spending as much time in the laboratory as with the books. She had learned about 'facials' and thought she could improve on the product and technique. In 1910, Florence met another beauty cream entrepreneur – Elizabeth Hubbard – who had already developed beauty creams and tonics. They decided to open an upscale salon on 5th Avenue where women could come for pampering. They would also market their own products through the 'Elizabeth Hubbard' salon.

The partnership did not work out – dissolving before the fledgling company had been launched.

Faced with abandoning her dream, Graham persevered alone. Instead of removing the fresh lettering on the door of the salon, she kept 'Elizabeth' and took the second name 'Arden' from her favourite Lord Tennyson poem, "Enoch Arden". She added 'Mrs.' for respectability and became Mrs. Elizabeth Arden. Called the "little Canadian woman with the magic hands" by her clients, she prospered.

Despite humble beginnings and two failed marriages (which hurt her financially), by 1944 Arden had one thousand different products and owned salons throughout the U.S. and Europe.

When she died in 1965, she left a fortune estimated at $40 million and was described by Fortune Magazine as having "earned more money than any other businesswoman in the history of the United States." As a self-made millionaire, she was not perhaps the richest woman in the world, but she had become extremely successful by anyone's measure. Her discipline and willingness not to give up as well as her commitment to her product – made her a leader indeed.

When we face disappointment because the future we mapped out for ourselves does not materialize, it is easy to give up and throw our dreams out the window. Obstacles, large and small, are often present between where we are and where we want to go. We can stay in bed, or we can pick ourselves up, brush ourselves off, and go on like the little Canadian woman with the magic hands.

17

COURAGE: FACE THE MUSIC

"My loving people, we have been persuaded by some, that are careful of our safety, to take heed how we commit ourselves to armed multitudes for fear of treachery; but I assure you, I do not desire to live to distrust my faithful and loving people... I have placed my chief strength and safeguard in the loyal hearts and good will of my subjects. And therefore I am come amongst you at this time, not as for my recreation or sport, but being resolved, in the midst and heat of the battle, to live or die amongst you all; to lay down, for my God, and for my Kingdom, and for my people, my honour and my blood, even the dust."

Queen Elizabeth I

In 1588, there was a danger that England would be invaded by Spain. The monarch of the time, Queen Elizabeth I came to visit her troops on the banks of the Thames River at Tilbury.

Although she had been advised that her own troops would be a danger to her, she believed it was more important to show them that she was there with them. Her courage and dedication to her country rallied those around her and they won the battle against Spain (more commonly referred to as The Spanish Armada).

To have a battle to win and to be advised that your own troops might kill you instead of the enemy, certainly would be an uncomfortable feeling. It would take courage to step forward and

risk your physical safety. In today's world, we are sometimes called upon to face our staff and shareholders when we need to announce layoffs or poor share performance. Those are the times when we can find a million things to do without having to leave our office or answer the phone. With voice messaging, we can put off facing the music indefinitely.

Courageous is the leader who looks his team members in the eye and addresses their trust and information issues. Courageous is the leader who can address issues from stakeholders and shareholders with élan, neither losing control nor empathy.

Great leaders are those that go beyond dealing with the issues of their performance as they arise. They take the step of asking how they are performing and listen carefully without defensiveness or anger.

We all say we want feedback on our performance – but do we really? We want to know the good stuff, not the bad. We want to hear how great a coach we are, not that we are a poor delegator. A good leader asks for feedback and a great one uses it.

As we climb the ladder of success (and office floors), we have a tendency to lose the humility that moved us up the first couple of steps. But one 360-degree feedback event, where we are anonymously evaluated by those we supervise, that supervise us and our colleagues could bring that all crashing down. Our inclination is to reject negative comments, belittle those who made them and go on our merry way. To shoot the messenger, so to speak, rather than be self-reflective and see what part of the problem is about us, is often our preferred action.

Great leaders respect those who have the courage to speak up and are courageous themselves by reflecting on how they can use that information to improve.

18

FINAL THOUGHTS

Were you shocked by the Disney song research? Surprised by how large the gender wage gap really is – and that it actually widens for women as they gain higher levels of education? Had you considered the imbalance of male representation in media power roles? Were you thinking that the influence of fairy tales disappeared from our lives once we donned our first pair of pantyhose?

Although women have made major gains in equality in society and the workplace, the data in this book shows us where there is still work to be done. Not only do we need to toss the tiara and abandon the crippling beliefs that fairy tales have given us, we need to make conscious decisions in how we act and think.

INDEX

APPENDIX

Song List from Research – Chapter Eight

Snow White and the Seven Dwarfs (1937) Some Day My Prince Will Come
Pinocchio (1940) When You Wish Upon a Star
Dumbo (1941) When I See an Elephant Fly
Bambi (1942) Love is a Song
Saludos Amigos (1942) Saludos Amigos
The Three Caballeros (1944) Three Amigos Song
Make Mine Music (1946) Make Mine Music
Fun and Fancy Free (1947) Fun and Fancy Free
Melody Time (1948) Melody Time
Cinderella(1950) A Dream is a Wish Your Heart Makes
Alice in Wonderland (1951)A Very Merry Unbirthday
Peter Pan (1953) You Can Fly
Lady and the Tramp (1955) Bella Notte
Sleeping Beauty (1959) Once Upon a Dream
101 Dalmatians (1961) Creulla De Ville
The Sword in the Stone (1963) The Sword in the Stone
The Jungle Book (1967) Bare Necessities
The Aristocats (1970) Everybody Want To Be a Cat
Robin Hood (1973) The Phony King of England
The Rescuers (1977) The Journey
The Many Adventures of Winnie the Pooh (1977) Winnie the Pooh
The Fox and the Hound (1981)Best of Friends
The Great Mouse Detective (1986) Goodbye So Soon
Oliver & Company (1988) Why Should I Worry
The Little Mermaid (1989) Part of Your World
Beauty and the Beast (1991)Beauty and the Beast
Aladdin (1992) A Whole New World
The Lion King (1994) Circle of Life
Pocahontas (1995) Colors of the Wind
The Hunchback of Notre Dame(1996) Out There
Hercules (1997) Go the Distance
Mulan (1998) I'll Make a Man Out of You
Tarzan (1999) Two Worlds, One Family

The Emperor's New Groove (2000) Walk the Llama Llama
Atlantis: The Lost Empire (2001) Where the Dream Takes You
Treasure Planet (2002) I'm Still Here
Brother Bear (2003) Look Through My Eyes
Home on the Range (2004) You Ain't Home on the Range
Meet the Robinsons (2007) We're the Kids of the Future
Bolt (2008) I Thought I Lost You
The Princess and the Frog (2009) Down in New Orleans
Tangled (2010) I See the Light
Wreck-It Ralph (2012) Sugar Rush

NOTES/REFERENCES

Introduction

"Gender Diversity in top management: moving corporate culture, moving boundaries" (Sandrine Devillard, Sandra Sancier, Charlotte Werner, Ina Maller, Ceceile Kossoff) Kinsey & Company, November 2013

Chapter 1

StatsCanada

Pay Equity Commission, Government of Ontario

Chapter 2

Why Gender Matters, Leonard Sax, MD, PhD, 2005.

"Why Are Most Drowning Victims Men? Sex Differences in Aquatic Skills and Behaviours," Jonathan Howland and Associates, American Journal of Public Health, 1996.

Women Don't Ask: Negotiation and the Gender Divide, Linda Babcock and Sara Laschever, 2003.

"Female Grads Make Less Than Males," Regina Leader Post, April 27, 2004

Statistics from 2014 data from StatsCanada

Chapter 5

All statistics from Statista.com

Chapter 7

Bonomi, Amy E.; Altenburger, Lauren E.; Walton, Nicole L. (September 2013). "Double crap! Abuse and harmed identity in Fifty Shades of Grey". *Journal of Women's Health* (Mary Ann Liebert, Inc.) 22 (9): 733–744. doi:10.1089/jwh.2013.4344. PMID 23931257.

Chapter 8

Academy of Pediatrics. (2009). Impact of music, music lyrics, and music video on children and youth. *Pediatrics, 124*(5), 1488-1494.

Eagly, A., & Johannesen-Schmidt, M. (2001). The leadership styles of men and women. *Journal of Social Issues, 57*(4), 781-797.

Eagly, A., & Karau, S. (2002). Role congruity theory of prejudice toward female leaders. *Psychological Review, 109*(3), 573-598.

Hoover, K., Pepper, M.B., & Topuzova, Name that tune: *A Study of Cultivating Gender and Leadership Roles Form the Lyrics of Snow White and Peter Pan, Tangled and Wreck It Ralph.*

Chapter 9

Number of men watching Sports stat:
http://www.hollywoodreporter.com/news/television-shows-men-watch-222356

Chapter 16

Miss Elizabeth Arden: An Unretouched Life by Alfred A. Lewis and Constance Woodworth.

ABOUT THE AUTHOR

Jeanne Martinson, M.A. is a professional speaker, trainer and best-selling author who has worked internationally and throughout Canada. Since co-founding her own firm, MARTRAIN Corporate and Personal Development in 1993, Jeanne has inspired thousands of participants in her workshops and keynote presentations with her humor, insight and real-world examples.

Jeanne became interested in training while working for a Fortune 500 company in southern California. Back in her home province of Saskatchewan, she side-stepped into sales and marketing for ten years in the printing and labelling industry, where she took a $25,000 sales territory and grew it to $850,000 within four years.

Jeanne completed her Master of Arts degree in Leadership at Royal Roads University in Victoria, British Columbia, Canada. (Her graduate research focused on the differences and similarities of criminal gang leaders and corporate leaders). Jeanne also holds a Certificate in Organisational (Organizational) Behaviour from Heriot-Watt University (Edinburgh, Scotland) and is certified as a practitioner of NLP (Neuro Linguistic Programming).

As Managing Partner of her own firm, Jeanne delivers workshops and keynote addresses to government, associations and the private sector. Her most popular topics are leadership and diversity. As a Canadian bestselling author and strategist in workplace diversity, Jeanne's goal is to assist leaders in understanding diversity issues so they may attract, retain and engage their ideal workforce.

In July 1999, Jeanne released her first non-fiction book titled *Lies and Fairy Tales That Deny Women Happiness* which explores the myths that many Canadian women are raised with and which limit their ability to have happy relationships and fulfilling careers.

Her second book, *Escape from Oz – Leadership For The 21st Century* was released in October 2001. This book explores the parallels of the characters in the fable *The Wonderful Wizard of Oz* and our own beliefs about personal and professional leadership.

Jeanne's third book, *War & Peace in the Workplace – Diversity, Conflict, Understanding, Reconciliation* was released September 2005. This book explores how workplaces are becoming more diverse and how diversity may trigger conflict. The book illustrates how we have the choice of allowing conflict to spiral down into dysfunction or of taking charge, becoming aware and developing understanding.

Jeanne's fourth book was a chapter based on her graduate work in a larger compilation. Her research was published by the International Leadership Association in their annual journal (2012) as a peer-reviewed journal article (Leadership Lessons from the Criminal World).

Jeanne's fifth book, *Generation Y and the New Ethic,* was released Spring 2013. It gives concrete information about the four different generations found in the workplace today with a focus on work ethic and the motivations and values of Generation Y.

Jeanne's sixth book, *If it Wasn't for the Money,* is her first fiction novel and introduces her main character, Sam Anderson, a travel journalist and accidental murder detective. It was introduced in 2014.

Jeanne's seventh book, *Hemingway or Twain? Unleashing Your Author Personality,* is a book to help non-fiction book authors get their book completed with less stress, time and money.

Jeanne takes a leading role in her community, a dedication that was recognized with the awarding of the Canada 125 Medal, the YWCA Women of Distinction Award (Business, Labor and Professions), the Centennial Leadership Award (for outstanding contribution to the Province of Saskatchewan), the Athena Award, and the EMCY (the national Diversity award of Canada).

Jeanne has been listed in Who's Who of Canadian Women since 1996 and Canadian Who's Who since 1999. Jeanne is Past President of: Saskatchewan Training and Development Association (Regina Chapter), Saskatchewan Business and Professional Women, and Women Entrepreneurs of Saskatchewan. She was Founding President of the Saskatchewan Chapter of the Canadian Association of Professional Speakers (CAPS).

BOOKS BY
JEANNE MARTINSON

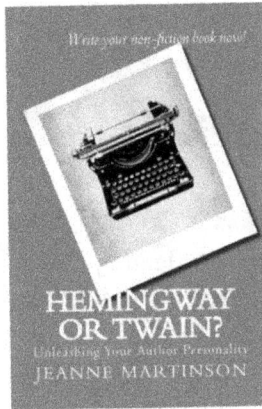

Hemingway or Twain? Unleashing Your Author Personality

Written by Jeanne Martinson
On KINDLE and available in print through Amazon

Not making any progress on writing your non-fiction book? Too much advice from too many people but none of it seems to work for you? The first step to success as an author is to identify your Author Personality. With this knowledge, you can save yourself frustration, time and money.

After identifying the answers to the key questions that determine your Author Personality, apply them to the Ten Step Book Project Model and to ensure completion of your book.

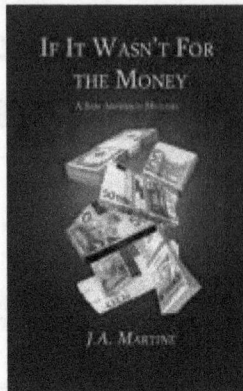

If It Wasn't For the Money
Written by Jeanne Martinson
Under the name J.A. Martine

On KINDLE and available through Amazon

Sailing on a cruise ship to Alaska to discover unusual adventures to write about for her magazine, OOTA, journalist Sam Anderson gets caught up in the disappearance of a wealthy dining companion.

Who could financially benefit from the death of the heiress? Travelling from the icy glaciers of Alaska to the steamy heat of New Orleans, Sam begins to tie up the loose strings of the mystery – but can she solve the puzzle before she too becomes a target?

(This is the first book in the Sam Anderson series. The second book, *Stay out of the Water,* is due out July 2016.)

Generation Y and
the New Work Ethic
Jeanne Martinson, MA

Generation Y
and the New Work Ethic

Available on KINDLE and inn print through Amazon

Every generation has rebelled against the norms of the generation preceding it. This rebellion manifests itself externally in clothes, hairstyles, temporary and permanent markings and maskings. As time passes, often these visual distinctions are toned down or abandoned as that generation ages and begins to fit into mainstream work worlds, eventually falling for the tie and pantyhose cultural norms of the workplace. Many of today's Generation Y cohort members may yet desert their desire for T-shirts and casual attitudes as they progress in their careers and organizations.

Managers ask me frequently "When will Gen Ys will grow up, quit rebelling and get with the program?" Unfortunately for managers and co-workers everywhere, there is more to generational difference than rebellion and a desire to be different from the previous generation. Our generational identity is also about the beliefs and values that were developed in our growing up years. By the time we hatch into the workforce, our perspectives of others, work and the world are well formed.

So why are we talking about generational differences now more so than in the past? Why has this last generation upset the apple cart so significantly? Because it is the perfect storm!

If you are a colleague trying to understand your multi-generational co-workers, a front line manager trying to get your youngest workers to show up and show up on time, or are a member of Generation Y and looking for ways to maximize your effectiveness and success in the workplace, this book gets to the heart of the generational differences issue, with minimal psychobabble and statistical navel gazing, giving you concrete information about the different generations with a focus on work ethic and the motivations and values of Generation Y.

Table of Contents

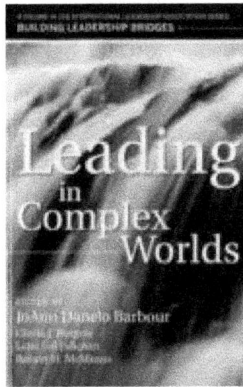

Leading in Complex Worlds

Chapter 8 – Leadership Lessons from the Criminal World – written by Jeanne Martinson

Available in print format from Wood Dragon Books

Released June 2012 by publisher Jossey-Bass, this collection of chapters from leadership experts and scholars is the annual peer-reviewed journal of the International Leadership Association. It contains chapters from fifteen authors, including a chapter by Jeanne Martinson titled "Leadership Lessons from the Criminal World" **which is based on her Master of Arts research project that compared criminal and corporate leaders.**

The other chapters include:

- Black Women's Political Leadership Development: Recentering the Leadership Discourse

- Soccer Tactics and Complexity Leadership

- The Role of Culture and History in the Applicability of Western Leadership Theories in Africa

- A Tao Complexity Tool, Leading from Being

- The Leadership of Dr. Jane Goodall: A Four Quadrant Perspective

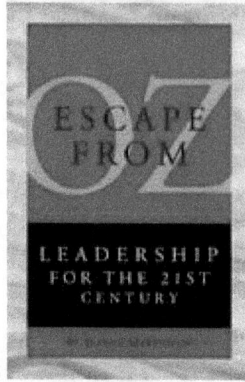

Escape from Oz – Leadership for the 21st Century

by Jeanne Martinson

Available in print and audio book at Wood Dragon Books

Available in KOBO and KINDLE eBook formats

This book explores the parallels of the characters in the fable *"The Wonderful Wizard of Oz"* and our own beliefs about personal and professional leadership.

The first part of the book explores the four cornerstones required to be an effective leader: courage, insight, self-discipline and influence over others.

The second part of the book explores how we can move out of our comfort zone to lead individuals according to their reality, skill set and knowledge base – with the goal of achieving trust and long term success.

This book, about the basics of personal leadership and leading others, is written to assist you in becoming an effective leader – whether you are leading an organization of two or two thousand.

Table of Contents

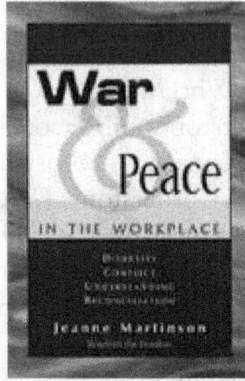

War & Peace
(Diversity, Conflict,
Understanding, Reconciliation)

by Jeanne Martinson

Available in print and audio book at Wood Dragon Books
Available at KOBO and KINDLE in eBook formats

Wonder why we can't just get along? Why we react to each other the way we do?

Most conflict in the workplace comes from our differences – both our diversity in the big 'D' issues such as race, gender or ability but also diversity in the small 'd' issues such as values, marital and family status, age or thought processes. Diversity can be problematic and it can be wonderful. As individuals and organizations, we can benefit from the many perspectives that create the synergy to move an organization forward by leaps and bounds.

On the other hand, differences can bring conflict, toxic work groups, low morale, harassment, misunderstandings and employee turnover.

Many organizations adopt respectful workplace or harassment policies. But this isn't enough to realize the benefits of a diverse workforce or to minimize diversity-based conflict. We need to shift how we perceive and work with others. This book illustrates how we have the choice of allowing conflict to spiral down into dysfunction or of taking charge, becoming aware and developing understanding. It's all up to you!

Table of Contents

CONTACT INFO

Jeanne Martinson, MA
Diversity Strategist, Best-selling Author,
Professional Speaker

Website: **www.martrain.org**
Mobile: 1.306.591.7993
Office: 1.306.569.0388
Snail Mail: PO Box 1216,
Regina, Saskatchewan, Canada S4P2B4

**For more information on Jeanne Martinson's
topics for your next conference,
visit our website at
www.martrain.org**

www.ingramcontent.com/pod-product-compliance
Lightning Source LLC
Chambersburg PA
CBHW052213270326
41931CB00011B/2337